SLIME SORCERY

97 Magical Concoctions Made from Almost Anything —
Including Fluffy, Galaxy, Crunchy, Magnetic,
Color-Changing and Glow-in-the-Dark Slime

Adam Vandergrift
creator of Will It Slime?

Ulysses Press

Published in the United States by:
Ulysses Press
P.O. Box 3440
Berkeley, CA 94703
www.ulyssespress.com

ISBN: 978-1-61243-754-5
Library of Congress Control Number: 2017952136

Printed in Canada by Marquis Book Printing
10 9 8 7 6 5 4 3 2 1

Acquisitions editor: Casie Vogel
Managing editor: Claire Chun
Editor: Lauren Harrison
Proofreader: Shayna Keyles
Front cover design: what!design @ whatweb.com
Interior design and layout: what!design @ whatweb.com

Distributed by Publishers Group West

NOTE TO READERS: This book is independently authored and published
and no sponsorship or endorsement of this book by, and no affiliation
with, any trademarked brands or other products mentioned within is
claimed or suggested. All trademarks that appear in this book belong to
their respective owners and are used here for informational purposes
only. The author and publisher encourage readers to patronize the quality
brands mentioned in this book.

CONTENTS

INTRODUCTION

Why slime? It's a classic, easy-to-make activity that's fun for everyone. For kids, slime can spark an interest in science and chemistry. For an adult, it awakens that inner child. But for all ages, it's about having fun!

Even though slime isn't new, making and playing with slime has recently become a bona fide worldwide phenomenon. Some people enjoy inventing different types of slime. Some enjoy just watching the process, while others find the sounds and textures satisfying and relaxing.

Sometimes slime making is about the journey and not the destination. Avalanche Slime (page 114), a popular slime on Instagram, is one such slime journey. It gets its unique look by stacking two different types of slime in a jar and allowing them to settle. After a few days, the different slimes rise and fall creating an almost magical appearance. You can see this action on my YouTube channel; look for the Giant Avalanche Slime video.

This phenomenon is thanks in part to the Internet. In the fall of 2016 on YouTube and Instagram, a rise in slime began. By February 2017, reports of a glue shortage were hitting the Internet headlines, and even the nightly news. What can I say? We slimers use a lot of glue. People who couldn't find glue to make slime began buying slime from those who could. Many slime businesses exploded onto the market. Most of these purveyors of slime gained their popularity on Instagram. While Instagram posts focus more on the sounds and visuals of slime, most of the YouTube content is based on DIYs and challenges.

WHAT IS SLIME?

The basic recipe for slime has been around for decades. It all started in 1976 when slime was created and sold by a toy company. But once people found it was easy to make at home, they got much more creative with the different recipes and uses.

Many of the recipes in this book are variations of the classic recipe. I've included my Basic Slime recipes on page 19. They're the best starting point for familiarizing yourself with slime and a great base for inventing your own recipes.

However, slime has gone way beyond the basics. Many of the recipes in this book were inspired by other slime chefs, but many more came from trial and error.

My personal favorite slime is Magnetic Slime. By adding iron oxide powder or iron shavings to the recipe, you can bring your slime to life. All you need is a magnet to attract the iron. When the iron is attracted to the magnet, it pulls the slime with it, allowing you to make your slime dance and move. Set the magnet in front of the slime and watch with amusement as the slime "eats" the magnet, as seen in my "Giant Magnetic Slime" video.

Sometimes slime can come from the most unusual places. I'm not talking about the crisper drawer in your refrigerator or last week's leftovers. I'm referring to the bathroom. Whoa, whoa, whoa, don't go there—toothpaste guys, toothpaste! Some of my biggest videos on YouTube are toothpaste slime recipes. These are easy to make because they are made with products that you *hopefully* already have at home.

WILL IT SLIME?

Slime may be experiencing a resurgence in popularity, but I learned how to make it over 30 years ago. It was a basic glue and borax recipe we learned in science class. It was so exciting as a child to be able to create something fun out of household supplies that were otherwise boring. I felt like a real scientist. I remembered the experience as I grew up, and I would share this process with my niece and nephew, to their amazement. Once my own children became interested in science experiments and crafting, I showed it to them. They felt that same excitement I did as a child. Then they began asking to make it more and more often. To make a long story short, slime has taken over my life...well, part of it anyway.

I knew slime was trending when I started my YouTube channel, but I had no idea just how quickly the channel would take off. My wife and I now spend at least 30 hours a week elbow-deep in slime. My daughters love being involved in the videos, and even help us come up with new ideas. We're constantly testing new recipes, filming, editing, and posting new videos online. I love interacting with my fans and subscribers. I am so grateful for them.

SLIME SCIENCE

How does slime become slime? What makes it ooze and goo, pop and stick? It's all in the science.

Technically, slime is a liquid. Even though it feels solid, it will still eventually take the shape of any container you put it in, and that's how you know it's a fluid. But it's not the same kind of liquid as water or oil, or even shampoo.

There are two main types of fluids: the Newtonian fluids, like water, and the non-Newtonian fluids, like slime. To understand what that means, you're going to have to understand a concept called viscosity. Basically, a fluid's viscosity is its resistance to flow. The viscosity of Newtonian fluids is only affected by heat, but the non-Newtonian fluids can change viscosity for other reasons.

Water, a Newtonian fluid, is usually not very viscous. Think of a water bottle. When you tip it upside-down to empty out the water, the water will just pour right out! Now, what happens if you put the water bottle in the freezer for a few hours? If you try to pour the water out, it won't work: The viscosity has changed because the water is frozen.

Heat isn't the only thing that affects liquids like slime. Shear stresses, or forces, can change the viscosity of non-Newtonian liquids. Here's an example: Imagine you have a ball of Silly Putty and you stretch it really slowly. It won't break! Now imagine pulling on it really hard. If you pulled hard enough, the silly putty will snap in half, almost like it's solid. In the first example, the Silly Putty became less viscous; in the second, it became more viscous.

Slime gets its non-Newtonian properties from its most basic ingredient: glue. There are other ingredients, or "slime activators," that you can use (see the Shopping List on page 15). In this book, they are mainly liquid laundry detergent (Tide and Gain), liquid starch (Sta-Flo), salt, and contact lens solution combined with baking soda.

Glue is a polymer, which means it's made of long chains of molecules. These chains of molecules collide and flow over each other, which is what makes glue both flexible and somewhat slow-moving. When you add an activator to glue, a chemical reaction takes place that connects all of the polymer chains together. This makes it harder for them to flow over each other, but they still stay flexible. They stop acting as a Newtonian liquid, and start acting like slime!

SLIME SAFETY

Not all slimes are alike. Simple slime recipes can be made by using only two ingredients, but by adding other ingredients you can change the texture and appearance, giving you multiple outcomes. A good example of this is Fluffy Slime, a lighter, bouncier slime created by adding shaving cream to the basic slime recipe.

You can also make slimes that are safe to eat. I know, that sounds crazy, but it's true! Edible slimes can be made by using marshmallows, Marshmallow Fluff, or a Metamucil base. Add in some tasty treats, flavoring, or your favorite candy, and you have a delicious-tasting edible slime. If you're feeling hungry and adventurous you may want to try out some of these delectable recipes.

Of course, make sure you follow safe handling practices when making slime. Here are a few things to keep in mind:

- Children should always make slime with adult supervision.

- Keep any non-natural substances away from the face when making slime to prevent irritating the eyes and nose.

- Do not eat any slime that is not specifically listed as edible.

- Remember to wash your hands thoroughly after making and playing with slime.

If you're having trouble with your slime, check out the Slime FAQs (page 13) for some tips.

HOW TO USE THIS BOOK

All the slime recipes I've mentioned here and many more are included in this book, each with step-by-step instructions and color photos. The book is broken up into six different slime categories. First, we'll start with the basics. These are the recipes you'll want to master first.

Next is Sensory Slimes. These are all about the "crunch" and "squish" factors of slime. Each of these slimes create a fun sensory explosion, either with sound or texture.

After that, we talk about Food-Inspired Slimes. These look like food, smell like food, or taste like food! A handful are edible (this will be indicated next to the title), but please make sure before eating that you don't have any allergies.

Glitter Slimes are the next category. This is where we get really serious about glitter, sparkle, and shine. Fantastical slimes in this category range from unicorn-inspired to the entire cosmos.

Even though most slimes use glue, there are a few that don't! The Glue-Free Slimes chapter includes some inventive creations that go beyond glue and incorporate some weird and fun ingredients.

The last category, but certainly not the least, is Viral Slimes. These are the slimes you may have seen dominating the internet. From Lava Slime to Glow-in-the-Dark Slime, these are the most popular slimes out there.

WHAT DO YOU DO WITH SLIME?

Slime is all about fun! There are tons of things you can do with slime, but here are some of my pro-tips for playing with slime, whether you're at home or starting your own Instagram or YouTube channel.

Slime Poking

Poking slime is a slimer's favorite way to play with their creations. The sound it makes when you poke the slime with one or all of your fingers and bring them out again is so satisfying.

Folding Slime

Folding slime is also fun. Start from the outside of your slime and fold one section to the middle. Do this all around your slime until you end up where you started, then repeat or poke.

Popping Slime

Popping slime sounds so nice. This works really well if you are playing with an airy slime such as Fluffy Slime. Take the slime between your hands and give it a squeeze. Hear the bubbles just burst over and over again.

Swirling Slime

Swirling your slime can be satisfying too. Make your swirl, then either begin poking it, popping it, or folding it. Actually, just do all three! Welcome to slimer heaven.

To get the perfect swirl:

Step 1: Stretch your slime between your hands until it is flexible and lines form in your slime.

Step 2: Gather the two ends of your slime into one hand and let your slime begin to fall.

Step 3: Let the falling slime touch the surface you were working on and move it forward, back, and around in a circular motion.

That's it! It takes a little practice but once you've got it, it's easy!

Regardless of which slimes you make first, you'll find that the possibilities for slime are virtually limitless. All you need is some imagination, creativity, and a zest for fun. Well, you might also need some glue, shaving cream, or toothpaste (see my Shopping List on page 15). I hope that after reading this book, you are inspired to create your own new recipes. Next time you're walking through your favorite grocery or craft store, you may find yourself looking at the products on the shelf and wondering, "Will it slime?"

Thanks, and happy sliming!

SLIME FAQS

My slime is too sticky, what do I do?

You can use a mixture of ½ teaspoon baking soda and 2 tablespoons water. You can also use a little baby oil.

Help! My slime won't stretch.

No worries. Just add hand lotion, a few pumps at a time, until you reach your desired consistency.

For Clear Slime (page 20), add more water and let it set. It will absorb the water, giving it more stretch.

My slime is too watery, what can I do?

Simple! Continue adding activator until it reaches a slime consistency.

What's the best way to mix slime?

You can add color and glitter before you add your activator, or you can make your slime and then fold in your color or glitter.

Does slime smell good?

Not always, but you can add a variety of essential oil scents to your slimes to heighten your slime-playing experience.

How do you keep slime after you make it?

If you want to keep your slime around for a while, you need to store it properly. You can use a sealed baggy or an airtight container.

How do I make my slime more colorful?

You can use many things to color your slime. Food coloring, paint, nail polish, and pigment powder are a few of your options.

How can I tell if my slime is edible?

Easy! Edible slime recipes in this book are identified as such beside their title. But in general, take a look at the ingredients you're using. Would you eat them? If the answer is no, go with your gut and keep it out of your mouth. Better safe than sorry!

How long does slime last?

If you use a high-quality, name-brand glue, like Elmer's, your slime should last weeks or even months, as long as you store it in an airtight container to keep it from drying out. Edible slimes will typically last one to three days.

Will slime stain my clothes?

As you might expect, I get slime in my clothes all the time. All you have to do is run the clothing under water before the slime dries and it will easily come out. I have been completely covered in slime and still saved my clothes numerous times.

Can kids make slime by themselves?

Many slimes in this book are safe for older children to make on their own or with minimal adult supervision. However, some include more dangerous materials or the use of a microwave and will require a grown-up to help out. Those projects note this.

SHOPPING LIST

These are the basic ingredients you'll need to make most of the awesome slimes in this book. Some of the more adventurous slimes may require additional materials not listed here.

Clear glue. Any liquid clear glue, such as Elmer's Liquid School Glue.

Clear white glue. Any liquid white glue, such as Elmer's Liquid School Glue.

Clear liquid laundry detergent. This is a slime activator. It's important that this detergent is clear. However, not all clear detergent works. I've had success using Tide and Gain products.

Sta-Flo liquid starch. This is another slime activator.

Contact lens solution. When mixed with baking soda, this will act as a slime activator. Any brand works, as long as the solution contains boric acid.

Clear, liquid peel-off face mask. This is a substitute for glue. You can find them in individual .33-ounce packets at most drug stores.

Baby powder. This will give your slime a matte finish and a fresh smell.

Cornstarch. This gives your slime a matte finish and a dense texture.

Baby oil. This helps take out extra stickiness from your slime.

Baking soda. Baking soda is very important for slime-making. Mixed with contact lens solution, it creates a slime activator. Mixed with water, it will help make slime less sticky.

Essential oils. Essential oils make your slime smell amazing.

Food coloring. Using food coloring allows you to add color to your slime and gives your eyes something exciting to look at.

Shaving cream. Pumps up your slime and makes it bouncier.

Foaming hand soap. Pumps up your slime and makes it bouncier.

Hair mousse. Pumps up your slime and makes it bouncier, while also adding a little more crunch.

Plastic crunchy items. Plastic decorative beads, plastic gems, and pony beads are some great examples of "crunchy" items that you can add to slimes for a textured crunch.

Styrofoam beads/balls, white and colored. Used to make Floam Slime (page 23), among other slimes.

Sealable plastic containers. These save your slime from an untimely death. Sealable plastic bags work too.

Various bowls for mixing. Make sure you have a number of bowls on hand for mixing your slime ingredients. Maybe don't use the one handed down from your great-great-grandmother, and stick with basic plastic ones. Keep in mind that food coloring could stain a bowl made from a porous material.

Spoons for mixing. Basic spoons you have in your kitchen work well. You should probably avoid dipping into the silver you save for holiday dinners.

THE BASICS

Basic Slime #1

In 1976, Mattel introduced Basic Slime to American kids. Since then, slime has expanded beyond just child's play. You'll see it used in schools as a science experiment, as a relaxation tool to reduce anxiety, or simply as a creative outlet. One thing remains a constant, though—slime continues to bring great satisfaction to those who play with it.

1 (4-ounce) bottle white glue

2½ tablespoons clear liquid detergent

medium bowl

spoon

1. Empty the white glue into a bowl. Now slowly add the detergent, continuously mixing with a spoon.

2. Once your slime is thoroughly mixed and holds it shape, pick it up and begin kneading it by hand. As you stretch the slime, it will become less sticky.

3. Store in a sealable container

Slime Hack

If your slime is too sticky, add a little more detergent.

Add a few drops of green food coloring for that classic slime look.

Basic Slime #2

Simple slime in just a few minutes—perfect!

½ tablespoon baking soda

1 tablespoon contact lens solution

1 (4-ounce) bottle white glue

small bowl

spoon

medium bowl

1. Mix the baking soda and contact solution together in a small bowl. This will be your activator.

2. Empty the white glue into a medium bowl.

3. Slowly add your activator into the glue and mix them together with the spoon.

4. Once your slime is thoroughly mixed and holds it shape, pick it up and begin kneading it by hand until it becomes less sticky.

5. Store in a sealable container.

Clear Slime

Clear Slime is super versatile and can be used as a base for many other incredible slimes. You may also see this referred to as liquid glass or crystal-clear slime.

1 (4-ounce) bottle clear glue

¼ cup water

3 to 4 tablespoons clear liquid detergent

medium bowl

spoon

1. Mix the clear glue and water together in a medium bowl.

2. Slowly add the clear detergent, one tablespoon at a time, into your glue mixture while stirring. Continue adding detergent and mixing with a spoon.

3. When the glue mixture is thoroughly mixed and holds it shape, you'll know that it's fully formed (some water will still remain). Remove from the bowl and place on a flat, smooth surface. The mixture will be a little sticky. Knead gently with your hands until it becomes less sticky.

4. Place the slime in an airtight container and let sit for 3 to 5 days, or until it is clear and free of bubbles.

Slime Hack

If your Clear Slime isn't stretchy enough, add a tablespoon of water and let it sit for a day. The slime will absorb the extra water.

For thicker, putty-like slime, add more detergent.

Clear Face Mask Slime

Face masks plus slime equals awesomeness!

½ tablespoon baking soda

1¼ tablespoons contact lens solution

2 (.33-ounce) packets liquid, clear, peel-off face mask

1 teaspoon water

small bowl

medium bowl

spoon

1. Combine the baking soda and contact lens solution thoroughly in a small bowl. Set aside. This will be your activator.

2. Combine the 2 packets of face mask with the water in a medium bowl.

3. Add your activator to the face masks and mix until thoroughly combined.

4. Place the slime in an airtight container and let sit for 3 to 5 days, or until it is clear and free of bubbles.

CLEAR SLIME

SENSORY SLIMES

Floam Slime

Add some texture to your slime with this tactile phenomenon. Styrofoam plus slime equals Floam Slime! This slime is stretchier than regular slime. And the tingly feeling you get when you squish Floam Slime between your hands and it crunches...it's a sensory overload!

1 (4-ounce) bottle white glue

3 drops food coloring of choice

2 cups shaving cream

3 tablespoons contact lens solution

1 to 2 cups small Styrofoam beads (2 to 4 mm)

medium bowl

spoon

1. Mix the white glue and food coloring in a medium bowl.

2. Add the shaving cream and mix all the ingredients together.

3. Add the contact lens solution little by little into the mixture, stirring thoroughly.

4. Once the slime is mixed thoroughly and holds it shape, but is still a little tacky, pour in your Styrofoam beads. Start with 1 cup and add more as desired for even more texture. Press and knead them in and enjoy.

5. Store in a sealable container.

Slime Hack

Instead of adding the Styrofoam beads to your slime, put them in their own bowl and pour the slime on top. It's a very satisfying variation!

Too sticky? Combine ½ teaspoon baking soda and 2 tablespoons water and apply to your slime as needed. This will get rid of the stickiness.

Fun Fact

Let your floam sit for a while and the Styrofoam beads will rise to the top.

Crunchy Surprise Ball

Surprise! This slime looks so ordinary until you reveal the beautiful center.

1 (4-ounce) bottle clear glue

¼ cup water

a few drops food coloring of choice (optional)

3 to 4 tablespoons clear liquid detergent

2 to 3 cups Styrofoam micro beads (1 to 2 mm)

2 tablespoons glitter

medium bowl

spoon

plastic wrap

1. Combine the glue, water, and food coloring, if using, in a medium bowl. Mix thoroughly.

2. Add the detergent 1 tablespoon at a time. Stir. You want to leave your slime slightly sticky.

3. Let it rest in the bowl at room temperature, covered with plastic wrap, for 3 to 5 days until the bubbles disappear.

4. When the bubbles are gone, begin adding the micro beads by pushing and kneading them into your slime. Add as many as will fit without falling out.

5. Roll your floam into a ball.

6. Take your pointer finger and push lightly into the ball to create a small hole. Put the glitter inside the hole and then close it up by pinching the sides of the ball back together.

7. Once you pull and stretch your crunchy floam ball, the surprise will be revealed, leaving you with a sparkling ball of floam. Surprise!

Slime Hack

Instead of glitter, try adding another kind of slime, gems, or even toys!

Ball Pit Slime

Jump in and get lost in this slime with its mass of color and crunch power. You won't want to put this energizing slime down!

1 recipe Clear Slime (see page 20)

1 cup colored Styrofoam balls, or as needed

medium bowl

1. After the Clear Slime has rested for 3 to 5 days, put it into a medium bowl and then add the Styrofoam balls.

2. Press the balls into your slime until no more will fit.

3. Shape the slime into a ball and enjoy the crunch it makes as you press and stretch it out.

Slime Hack

For the balls to stick the slime, it must be a little sticky.

Micro Bead Floam

Sensory heaven is found in these micro beads. Like the bigger versions, these Styrofoam beads create a wonderful feeling between your hands, but they provide an even fluffier experience.

1 (4-ounce) bottle white glue

2 cups shaving cream

2 to 3 teaspoons lotion

a few drops food coloring of choice (optional)

3 to 4 tablespoons clear liquid detergent

2 to 3 cups Styrofoam micro beads (1 to 2 mm), or as needed

medium bowl

spoon

1. Combine the glue, shaving cream, lotion, and food coloring, if using, in a medium bowl. Mix together thoroughly with a spoon.

2. Add the detergent 1 tablespoon at a time while mixing. You want to leave your slime slightly sticky, so avoid adding too much detergent.

3. Begin adding the micro beads by pushing and kneading them into your slime. Add as many as will fit without falling out.

Slime Hack

Instead of adding micro beads to your slime, place them inside a bowl and lower your slime into the mass of Styrofoam beads.

Princess Floam Crunch

This slime packs a real punch that will give you princess-sized tingles down your spine! Crunch, crunch, crunch, ahhh...yes, that's a nice sound, even for a proper princess.

1 (4-ounce) bottle clear glue

¼ cup water

a few drops of pink food coloring (optional)

1 to 2 tablespoons glitter

3 to 4 tablespoons clear liquid detergent

1 to 2 packages white Styrofoam beads (2 to 4 mm)

medium bowl

spoon

1. Combine the glue, water, food coloring, if using, and glitter in a medium bowl and stir together.

2. Add the detergent 1 tablespoon at a time and mix. Once your slime has come together, it should be just a little sticky to the touch, so avoid adding too much detergent.

3. Let's make some crunch! Place your clear slime in a bowl and add the Styrofoam beads. Continue adding beads until you cannot add anymore without them falling out.

4. Press and knead them into your slime to make sure they are stuck to it.

5. Pick up your crunchy floam slime, shape it into a ball, and begin your crunchy utopia.

Kaleidoscope Crunchy Slime

Full of colors, shapes, textures, and a major crunch! This slime is a tactile explosion that will have you playing for hours on end, putting your senses on overdrive. Satisfaction guaranteed.

1 (4-ounce) bottle clear glue

¼ cup water

3 to 4 tablespoons clear liquid detergent

2 to 3 cups colorful plastic beads or gems, ¼ inch or smaller

medium bowl

spoon

1. Pour the glue and water into a medium bowl and mix to combine.

2. Add in the detergent and mix until the slime begins to form. Make sure it's still a little tacky to the touch.

3. Now add the colorful beads 1 cup at a time by kneading them in with your hands. Continue adding them until your slime is full of beautiful beads.

Slime Hack

If you have added all your beads, but your slime is still too sticky, mix a pinch of baking soda with a tablespoon of water and apply as needed by kneading it in with your hands.

Crunchy Slime

Do you hear that satisfying sound? That's the relaxing sound of Crunchy Slime, a favorite among the slime community. Once you start playing with this slime, you can't stop. Beware: It is highly addictive! It will have you tingling all the way to your toes. Note that the decorative beads used to make the crunch are sometimes referred to as "fishbowl beads" and are often used in the vases of artificial flower arrangements.

1 (4-ounce) bottle clear glue

¼ cup water

2 drops food coloring of choice

3 to 4 tablespoons clear liquid detergent

1 cup clear plastic decorative beads

medium bowl

spoon

1. Mix the clear glue, water and food coloring in a medium bowl.

2. Next, slowly add the detergent and stir to combine. Be sure not too add to much, as you want it to stay a little sticky.

3. Knead the slime by hand until it is mixed and holds it shape, but is still tacky.

4. Pour in the clear beads and press and knead them into the slime until they are evenly distributed.

Crunchy Millefiori Slime Ball

Mix up your favorite millefiori beads and make a crunch that is satisfying to the ears and visually stimulating to the eyes. Millefiori is a technique that produces decorative patterns in glass or clay. Millefiori beads made from polymer clay can be purchased online. You can also buy millefiori canes and cut your own beads (with adult supervision). You can't beat this picturesque creation!

1 (4-ounce) bottle clear glue
¼ cup water
3 to 4 tablespoons clear liquid detergent

1 to 2 cups millefiori beads
shallow dish
medium bowl
spoon

1. Pour the clear glue into a medium bowl and then add the water. Mix to combine.

2. Add the detergent a little at a time and combine the ingredients slowly until it comes together in a slime.

3. Remove the slime from the bowl and knead it with your hands on a flat surface. Knead until the slime is solid, but slightly sticky, which will help the millefiori beads stick to your slime. If your slime is completely white, you may want to let it rest in a sealed container for 3 to 5 days until it becomes clear.

4. Now let's make this slime crunchy! Place your clear slime into a shallow dish and begin adding in millefiori beads.

5. Fold them in with your fingertips. Continue adding them until your slime is full. Let the crunch fest begin!

Coal Miner Slime

Large lumps of crunch await you in this exciting slime. The diversity of its crunchiness is yours to explore.

medium pieces of Styrofoam

black water-based paint or food coloring, as needed

1 (4-ounce) bottle clear glue

¼ cup water

1 to 2 teaspoons hand lotion, any color

2 teaspoons cornstarch

½ cup hair mousse

¼ cup Sta-Flo liquid starch

large bowl

spoon

1. Start by breaking up your Styrofoam into chunks about ½ inch in size. Once you are satisfied with the sizes of the pieces, measure about 2 cups of the Styrofoam and color them with paint or food coloring until they are completely black. Set aside to dry.

2. Next, pour the clear glue into a large bowl and mix in the water.

3. Add the lotion, cornstarch, and mousse. Mix. Adding more lotion will make your slime stretchier.

4. After all the ingredients are combined, add the Sta-Flo. Stir until the mixture forms into slime and is no longer sticky.

5. Fold in the Styrofoam pieces by hand.

6. Knead with your hands. Begin exploring your coal mine and all the crunchy goodness it has to offer.

Papier-Mâché Slime

Slime that you can sculpt with? Doesn't get much cooler than that! This slime has a papery texture that is dense and smooth. When you're done playing with it, make a masterpiece and lay it out to dry. You can find CelluClay Instant Papier Mâché at most craft stores.

1 (4-ounce) bottle white glue

½ cup water

5 drops food coloring of choice

1½ to 2 cups CelluClay Instant Papier Mâché

3 to 4 tablespoons liquid detergent

medium bowl

spoon

1. Pour the glue, water, and color into a medium bowl and mix.

2. Add the CelluClay and mix again until it is a thick but stretchable consistency.

3. Once all ingredients are combined, add the detergent until the slime is no longer sticky and holds its shape.

Drying Your Slime

When you're ready to dry your slime sculpture, place it on a piece of parchment paper and then lay it on top of a cooling rack. Set the rack in the sun for a few hours. Slime masterpiece complete!

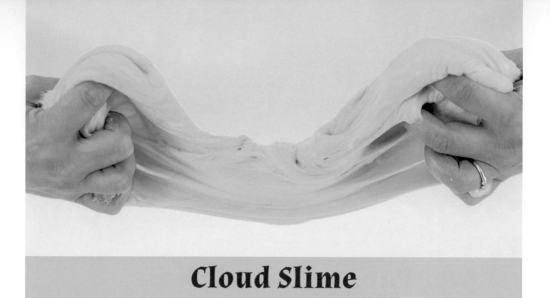

Cloud Slime

Did you know that clouds are crunchy? OK, real clouds aren't, but these slime clouds are. When you squeeze them they pop and crinkle with ease.

½ tablespoon baking soda

1¼ tablespoons contact lens solution

1 (4-ounce) bottle clear glue

2 drops food coloring of choice

1 cups hair mousse

1 cup shaving cream

small bowl

spoon

medium bowl

1. First, mix together the baking soda and contact lens solution in a small bowl; this is your activator.

2. Combine the glue, food coloring, mousse, and shaving cream in a medium bowl and mix to combine fully.

3. Add the activator and mix to combine.

4. When your slime is no longer sticky, it's time to play!

Sand Slime

This slime contains sand, but it's anything but sandy! It is smooth, thick, and moldable. Pure satisfaction!

1 (4-ounce) bottle clear glue

¼ cup water

½ cup colored crafting sand

8 teaspoons clear liquid detergent

medium bowl

spoon

1. Pour the glue into a medium bowl and then add the water. Mix to combine.

2. Add the sand and mix thoroughly.

3. Pour in the detergent and stir to combine all the ingredients.

4. Once your slime is mixed thoroughly and holds it shape, take it out, and knead it by hand until it is no longer sticky.

Madison's Sand Slime

Texture, texture, texture is what this slime is all about. Sensory heaven is found in this one-of-a-kind slime.

1 (4-ounce) bottle white glue
glitter, as much as desired
2 to 4 drops food coloring of choice
2 (8-ounce) packages Kinetic Sand

3 to 5 tablespoons Sta-Flo liquid starch
large bowl
spoon

1. Combine the glue, glitter, food coloring, and Kinetic Sand in a large bowl. Mix.

2. Begin adding Sta-Flo a little at a time, stirring constantly, until the slime begins to form.

3. Once your slime is fully mixed and holds it shape, take it out of the bowl and knead it between your hands until it is no longer sticky.

Madison's Whipped Sand

Whip up this textured sensory slime and you will have the best of both worlds: amazing texture and a fluffy fluff ball.

1 (4-ounce) bottle white glue
2 cups shaving cream
glitter, as much as desired
2 to 4 drops food coloring of choice

2 (8-ounce) packages Kinetic Sand
3 to 5 tablespoons Sta-Flo liquid starch
large bowl
spoon

1. Combine the glue and shaving cream in a large bowl. Mix to combine.

2. Next, add the glitter, food coloring, and Kinetic Sand. Mix to combine.

3. Add the Sta-Flo a little at a time, stirring constantly, until the slime begins to form.

4. Once your slime is mixed thoroughly and holds it shape, take it out of the bowl and stretch it between your hands until it's no longer sticky.

MADISON'S WHIPPED SAND

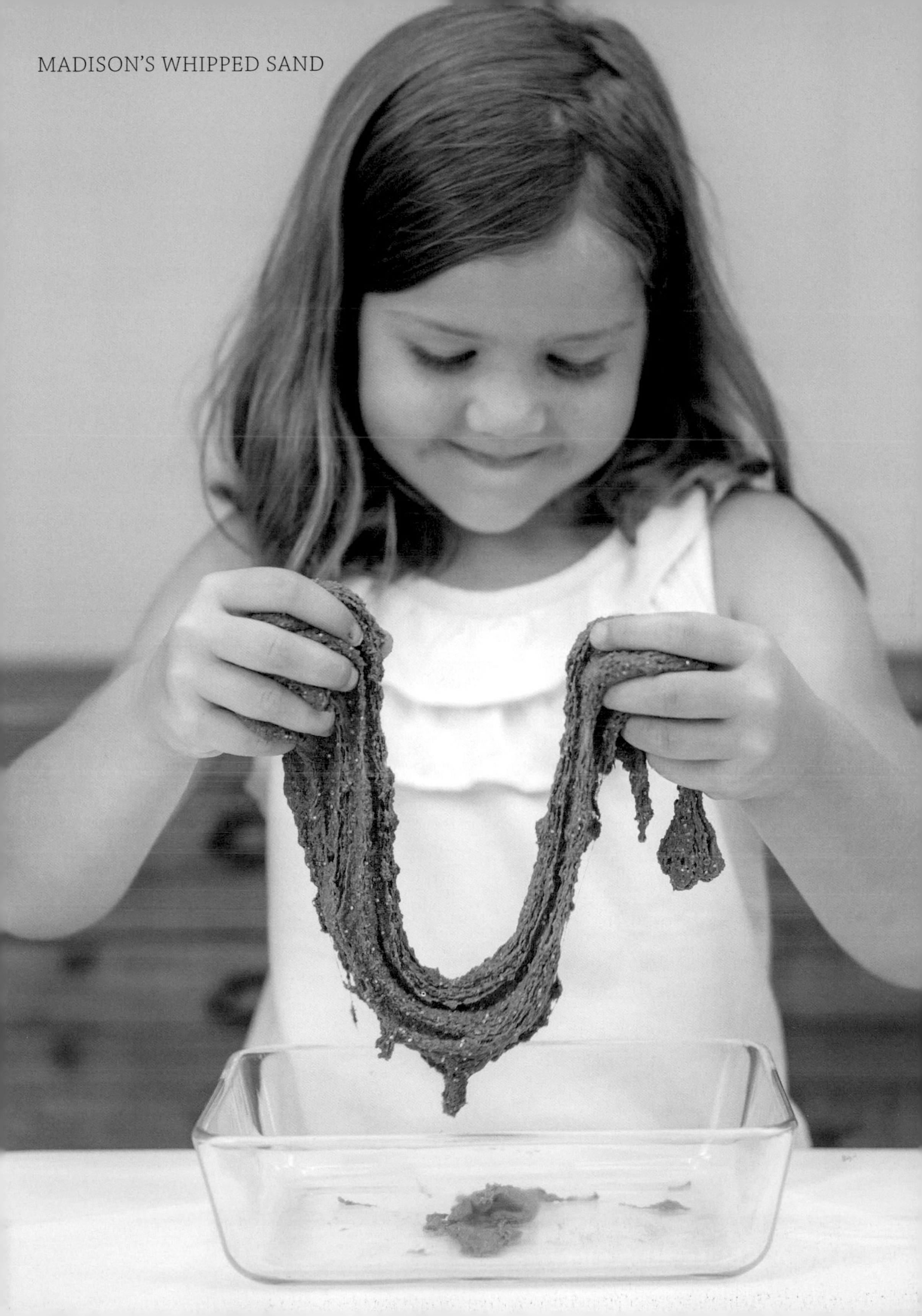

Riley's Crystal Slime

You have to think outside the box sometimes to achieve new and exciting results. This slime's unique appearance and texture take creativity to a whole new level.

1 disposable diaper

scissors

1 drop blue food coloring

¼ cup water

1 (4-ounce) bottle clear glue

3 tablespoons clear liquid detergent

medium bowl

spoon

1. Cut the diaper in half and release all the absorbent powder (sodium polyacrylate) into a medium bowl. Be sure to pick out and discard any diaper debris.

2. Add the food coloring and mix.

3. Add the water. This will plump up the powder and turn it into "crystals."

4. Add the glue to the mixture and mix.

5. Add the detergent to activate the slime and mix.

6. Keep mixing until your slime is no longer too sticky. Then pick it up and stretch it between your hands until it is no longer sticky.

Riley's Crystal Puff

Pump up the volume of this unique slime! The fluffiness of this crystal slime will have you feeling like royalty.

1 disposable diaper

scissors

2 to 3 drops food coloring of choice

¼ cup water

1 (4-ounce) clear glue

2 cups shaving cream

5 to 7 tablespoons clear liquid detergent

2 medium bowls

spoon

1. Cut the diaper in half and release all the absorbent powder (sodium polyacrylate) into a medium bowl. Be sure to pick out and discard any diaper debris.

2. Now add the food coloring and mix to combine.

3. Add the water. This will plump up the powder and turn it into "crystals."

4. In a second medium bowl, stir together the glue and shaving cream.

5. Add the glue and shaving cream mixture to the first bowl and mix to combine.

6. Add the detergent to activate your slime, stirring to combine, until the slime forms and begins to hold its shape.

7. When your slime has come together, pick it up and stretch it with your hands until it is no longer sticky.

Snow Slime

If you've ever lived where it snows, you know how cold but beautiful it can be. Snow Slime isn't cold, but it does have the magical, shimmery look of real snow. Have fun with this wintery delight!

1 disposable diaper

scissors

¼ cup water

1 (4-ounce) bottle clear glue

2 cups shaving cream

5 to 6 tablespoons clear liquid detergent

iridescent glitter (optional)

2 medium bowls

spoon

1. Cut the diaper in half and release all the absorbent powder (sodium polyacrylate) into a medium bowl. Pick out and discard any diaper debris.

2. Add the water and stir until all water is absorbed. This will plump up the powder and turn it into "crystals."

3. In a second medium bowl, mix together the glue and shaving cream.

4. Next, add your absorbent powder mixture (snow) to your glue mixture and stir them together.

5. Activate your slime by adding the detergent until it starts to form a slime, stirring to combine.

6. Knead and stretch your slime in your hands until it is completely mixed and holds it shape.

Slime Hack

Mix ½ teaspoon baking soda with 2 tablespoons water, and knead it into your slime to help lessen stickiness.

FOOD-INSPIRED SLIMES

Confetti Birthday Cake Slime

You will be so excited to play with this bright and happy slime. Rich in color and texture, it's the perfect birthday surprise!

½ tablespoon baking soda

1¼ tablespoons contact lens solution

1 (4-ounce) bottle white glue

2 cups shaving cream

1 to 2 tablespoons lotion

5 to 7 drops yellow food coloring

1 to 2 cups large and small colored Styrofoam balls

medium bowl

small bowl

spoon

1. In a small bowl, stir together the baking soda and contact lens solution. This is your activator.

2. In a medium bowl, add the glue, shaving cream, lotion, and food coloring, and stir to combine. The more lotion you add, the more stretchy your slime will be.

3. Add your activator to the glue mixture.

4. Mix until all the ingredients are combined thoroughly and your slime holds it shape. The slime should be slightly sticky.

5. Now fold the Styrofoam balls into your slime, and knead them in with your hands until all the Styrofoam balls stick into your slime.

Slime Hack

If your slime is still too sticky, mix ½ teaspoon baking soda and 2 tablespoons water, and knead it into your slime to help lessen stickiness.

Buttercream Frosting Slime

The rich, smooth, and creamy feel of buttercream frosting does not go unnoticed with this airy slime. Even the smell will have you wishing you could eat it! (But don't eat it.)

1 (4-ounce) bottle white glue

5 drops food coloring of choice

2 drops vanilla essential oil

2 cups shaving cream

6 to 7 tablespoons Sta-Flo liquid starch

2 cups white Crayola Model Magic soft clay

medium bowl

spoon

1. Thoroughly combine the glue, food coloring, essential oil, and shaving cream in a medium bowl.

2. Begin pouring in the Sta-Flo and mix until it comes together into a slime and begins to hold its shape.

3. Once all the Sta-Flo is incorporated and your slime holds it shape, begin kneading in the clay. You should end up with a creamy Buttercream Frosting Slime.

Slime Hack

Top your frosting with glitter, colored Styrofoam balls, or any kind of confetti to give it a celebratory look.

Sherbet Slime

This slime is packed full of vibrant colors and fragrances. You can make it however you like: orange, lemon, vanilla, lime. The possibilities are endless.

¼ cup Clear Slime (see page 20)

3 to 4 drops food coloring of choice

½ cup white Crayola Model Magic soft clay

1 or 2 drops essential oil of choice

medium bowl

spoon

1. Put your premade slime into a medium bowl and fold in the food coloring with a spoon.

2. Mix in the clay until your slime is nice and smooth, without any clumps remaining.

3. Fold in the essential oil.

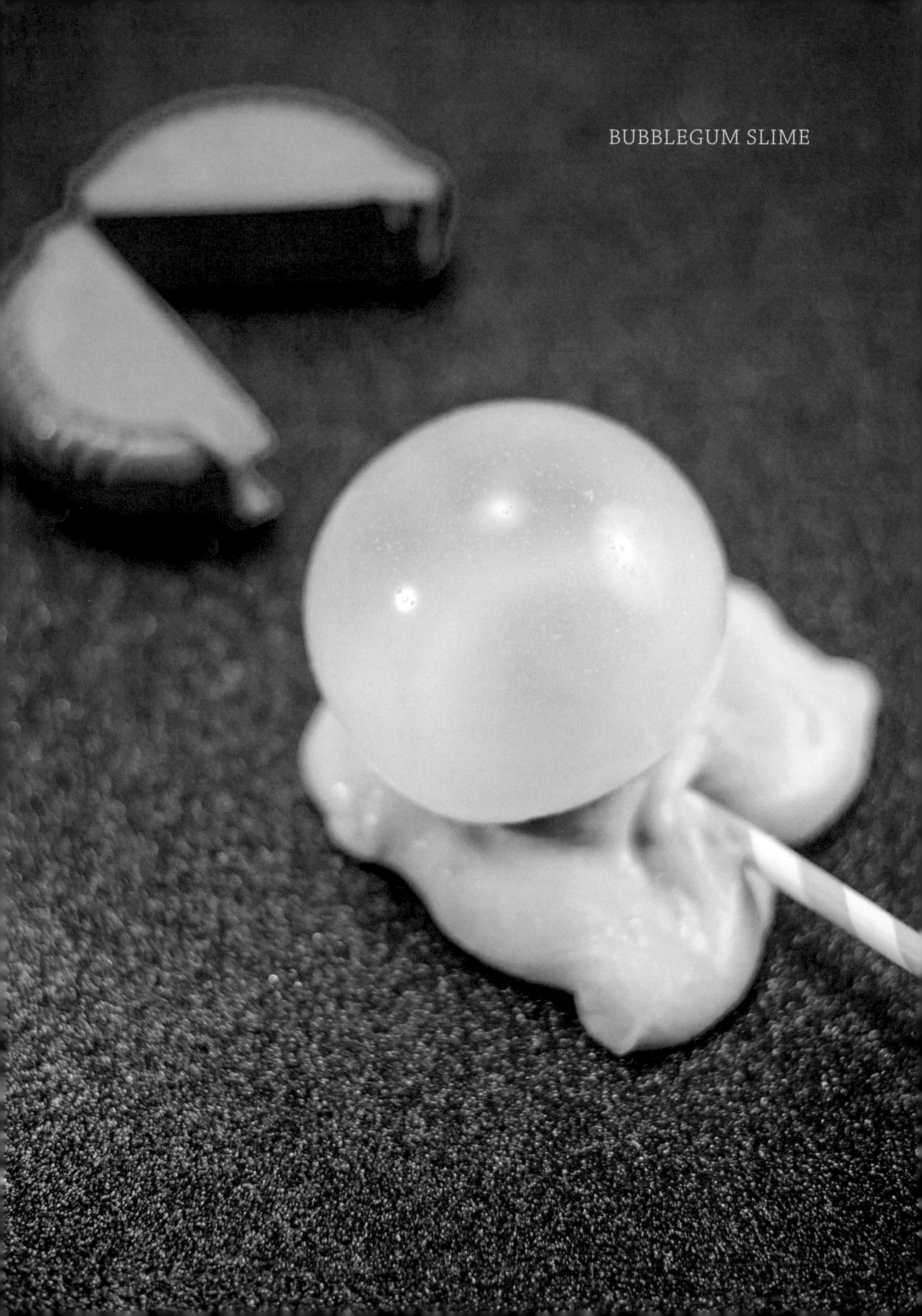

BUBBLEGUM SLIME

Bubblegum Slime

Slime you can actually blow bubbles with—how cool is that? So grab a straw and let's get to it.

1 (4-ounce) bottle white glue

1 drop red food coloring

¼ cup clear liquid detergent

straw

medium bowl

spoon

1. Pour the glue into the bowl and then add the food coloring. Mix thoroughly.

2. Next, add the detergent and mix until your slime is combined thoroughly and holds its shape.

3. Now, slide a straw into the middle of your slime and blow out until you see bubblegum bubbles.

Slime Hack

If your slime is still too sticky, mix ½ teaspoon baking soda and 2 tablespoons water, and knead it into your slime to help lessen stickiness.

Milky Slime

With a silky-smooth texture, this slime glides between your fingers and has the appearance of real milk.

1 (4-ounce) bottle white glue

¼ cup water

3 to 4 tablespoons Sta-Flo liquid starch

3 teaspoons lotion

medium bowl

spoon

1. Pour the glue into a medium bowl and add the water. Mix to combine.

2. Add the Sta-Flo and mix again.

3. Once the mixture is combined thoroughly, begin kneading the lotion in with your hands until the slime stretches without tearing.

Slime Hack

Let your slime sit in water for a few minutes for a runnier consistency.

Cereal Slime

Fooling people is a favorite pastime, and so much fun to do. With this realistic slime, you will have the upper hand when it comes to pranking your family and friends. They won't believe their eyes!

1 recipe Milky Slime (see page 47)

30 colorful plastic ring beads (these should resemble Froot Loops) or colorful Styrofoam balls

cereal bowl

spoon

1. Place the milky slime into a cereal bowl and top it off with bead rings or Styrofoam balls.

2. Use a spoon to scoop up and play with this delicious looking slime.

Caution

It looks so realistic you may want to eat it, but don't. Let it sit out for a while and it will still look real. It's craziness!

Vanilla Soft-Serve Slime

This vanilla soft serve is smooth, silky, and satisfying to the touch. Add in a little vanilla scent and you may just want to eat this slime, but don't! It's just for fun.

1 (4-ounce) bottle white glue

2 cups shaving cream

4 to 5 teaspoons lotion

2 or 3 drops vanilla essential oil

6 to 7 tablespoons Sta-Flo liquid starch

¼ cup cornstarch

medium bowl

spoon

1. Mix the glue, shaving cream, lotion, and vanilla essential oil together in a medium bowl.

2. Slowly add the Sta-Flo, mixing until the slime comes together.

3. Once your slime is fully mixed, take it out and stretch it between your hands until it is no longer sticky.

4. Knead in the cornstarch to give it that matte finish.

Chocolate Soft-Serve Slime

No matter how good it looks and smells, remember not to eat this chocolate slime!

1 (4-ounce) bottle white glue

2 cups shaving cream

4 to 5 teaspoons lotion

2 to 3 drops chocolate essential oil

10 drops brown food coloring

6 to 7 tablespoons clear liquid detergent

¼ cup cornstarch

medium bowl

spoon

1. Pour the glue, shaving cream, lotion, essential oil, and food coloring to a medium bowl and stir to combine. Add more lotion to make it stretchier.

2. Slowly add in the detergent, and stir until the slime comes together.

3. Once your slime is combined, take it out of the bowl and stretch it between your hands until it is no longer sticky.

4. Knead in the cornstarch until the slime has a matte finish.

Slime Hack

For a darker brown color, add more brown food coloring or even a drop or two of black food coloring to your finished slime.

Strawberry Soft-Serve Slime

Strawberry Soft-Serve Slime is refreshing to play with and full of fragrance—but remember not to take a bite!

1 (4-ounce) bottle white glue

2 cups shaving cream

4 to 5 teaspoons lotion

5 to 7 drops red food coloring

2 to 3 drops strawberry essential oil

medium bowl

spoon

6 to 7 tablespoons Sta-Flo liquid starch

¼ cup cornstarch

1. Pour the glue, shaving cream, lotion, food coloring, and strawberry essential oil in a medium bowl and mix to combine.

2. Slowly add the Sta-Flo, stirring constantly until your slime begins to form and holds its shape.

3. Once your slime is combined, take it out and stretch it between your hands until it is no longer sticky.

4. Knead in the cornstarch until your slime has a matte finish.

STRAWBERRY SOFT-SERVE SLIME

Neapolitan Soft-Serve Slime

What's better than chocolate, vanilla, or strawberry soft serve ice cream? All of them combined! You can't beat the stunning visual that they display or the wonderful aroma that they give off. This is the ultimate soft serve, full of rich and smooth goodness. It's exhilarating to play with!

1 recipe Strawberry Soft-Serve Slime (see page 50)

1 recipe Chocolate Soft-Serve Slime (see page 50)

1 recipe Vanilla Soft-Serve Slime (see page 49)

large clear container

1. Place your strawberry slime on the left side of your container.

2. While holding it in place, add your chocolate slime in the middle.

3. Next, hold your chocolate in place and add in your vanilla slime.

4. That's it! Isn't it beautiful? Play with your Neapolitan Soft-Serve Slime now, or let it set for 1 to 5 days and allow the bubbles to rise to the top and then pop them.

Marshmallow Fluff Slime

Much like the real thing, this slime is silky, smooth, and shiny. It can be the base for many exciting recipes or easily stand alone.

2 (4-ounce) bottles white glue

3 cups shaving cream

1 cup foaming hand soap

4 tablespoons lotion

6 to 7 tablespoons contact lens solution

medium bowl

spoon

1. Combine the glue, shaving cream, soap, and lotion in a medium bowl and mix to combine.

2. Add the contact lens solution and mix until your slime begins to form.

3. Take your slime out of the bowl and stretch it between your hands until the slime is no longer sticky.

Slime Hack

If your slime is still sticky, mix ½ teaspoon baking soda and 2 tablespoons water together knead it into your slime. Voilà, stickiness is gone! If you don't have baking soda, you can also use 1 teaspoon baby oil to rid your slime of its sticky texture.

Peanut Butter Slime

Mmm...peanut butter. This slime looks, feels, and smells like the real thing—but be careful, because it's not, and definitely isn't edible. It is, however, smooth and creamy to the touch. If you have an allergy to peanuts, you can still enjoy this slime without adding the essential oil.

1 cup white Crayola Model Magic soft clay

3 cups shaving cream

1 drop peanut essential oil

8 to 10 drops brown paint

orange food coloring as needed

medium bowl

spoon

1. Place the clay in a medium bowl and fold in the shaving cream 1 cup at a time.

2. Mix in the essential oil.

3. Once your slime has come together, mix in the brown paint and orange food coloring until you reach that rich, peanut buttery color.

Crunchy Peanut Butter Slime

What's better than peanut butter? Crunchy peanut butter! Enjoy the smooth buttery feel of this slime with a little texture thrown in. You will go nuts with enjoyment! If you have an allergy to peanuts, you can still enjoy this slime without adding the essential oil.

1 cup small white Styrofoam balls (2 to 4 mm)

brown paint, as needed

paint brush

1 cup white Crayola Model Magic soft clay

3 cups shaving cream

1 drop peanut essential oil

orange food coloring as needed

medium bowl

small bowl

spoon

1. Place these Styrofoam balls in a small bowl and paint them brown (these will be the nuts). Let them sit for a few minutes until the paint has dried.

2. Place the clay in a medium bowl and fold in the shaving cream 1 cup at a time.

3. Mix in the essential oil.

4. Mix in 8 to 10 drops of brown paint and a little orange food coloring until you reach a rich peanut buttery color.

5. Once your slime has come together, is smooth, and you have the color that you desire, knead in the "nuts."

PEANUT BUTTER SLIME

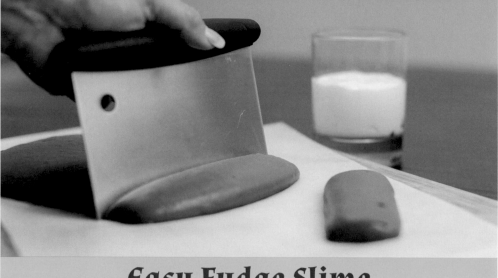

Easy Fudge Slime

The rich, creamy texture of this slime will make you hungry for the real thing (but careful—this one's not edible). Smooth and thick to the touch, this luxurious slime has a satisfyingly decedent chocolate aroma.

1 (4-ounce) bottle white glue

4 to 5 tablespoons brown paint

1 cup shaving cream

2 teaspoons lotion

2 or 3 drops chocolate essential oil

1 tablespoon cornstarch

2 to 3 tablespoons Sta-Flo liquid starch

2 cups white Crayola Model Magic soft clay, or as needed

medium bowl

spoon

1. Mix the glue, paint, and shaving cream in a medium bowl.

2. Mix in the lotion, essential oil, and cornstarch.

3. Activate your slime by adding the Sta-Flo. Once your slime starts to come together and is not overly sticky, take it out of the bowl and begin kneading it by hand.

4. When your slime is no longer sticky, start adding the clay. Knead in enough clay to achieve that fudge-like texture.

Slime Hack

Is your fudge too shiny? Knead in more cornstarch to your finished slime to give it a nice matte finish.

Add more brown paint for a darker fudge.

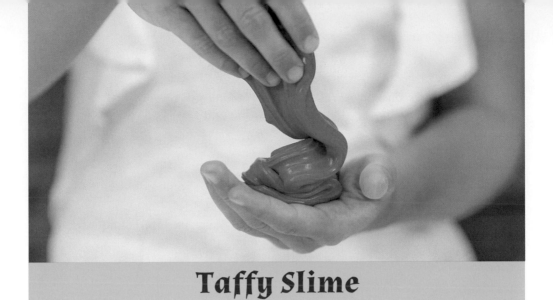

Taffy Slime

This two-step food-inspired slime is super easy to make and fun to play with!

¼ cup Clear Slime (see page 20)

3 to 4 drops food coloring of choice

1 or 2 drops essential oil of choice (optional)

¼ cup white Crayola Model Magic soft clay

small bowl

spoon

1. In a small bowl, mix together the Clear Slime, food coloring, and essential oil, if using.

2. Fold in the clay until the slime becomes smooth.

S'mores Slime

Just like real s'mores, this slime is full of delicious looking layers, which give it a satisfying realistic depth that might have you doing a double-take. I know you'll want to, but remember: Don't eat it!

brown paint

black paint

1 cup white Crayola Model Magic soft clay, divided

1 (4-ounce) bottle white glue

2 cups shaving cream

2 teaspoons lotion

2 to 3 teaspoons cornstarch

1 drop marshmallow essential oil (optional)

6 to 7 teaspoons Sta-Flo liquid starch

medium bowl

spoon

MAKE THE GRAHAM CRACKERS AND A CHOCOLATE BAR

1. First, fold the paint into the clay. Make one-fourth of the clay tan and one-fourth of the clay dark brown. To make a dark brown, add a drop of black paint into your clay and fold it in.

2. Now roll both clay colors into ¼-inch-wide squares. Press graham cracker designs into the tan squares so they look more realistic.

3. Set all of the squares aside to harden slightly.

MAKE SOME GOOEY MARSHMALLOWS.

1. In a bowl, mix together the white glue, shaving cream, lotion, cornstarch, and marshmallow essential oil, if using.

2. Next, pour in the Sta-Flo and mix until your slime comes together and holds its shape.

3. Knead in the remaining ½ cup of white clay.

S'MORES TIME!

1. Assemble your slime s'mores. Start with a tan square on the bottom (graham cracker) and top it with your dark brown square (chocolate).

2. Add some of your gooey white slime (marshmallow), and top it off with another tan square (graham cracker).

Slime Hack

If you happen to end up with leftover clay, make more s'mores.

Salted Caramel Slime

Mmmm, who's hungry? Salted caramel is a favorite among many people, and now it's a slime too. Stretch it, pop it, just don't eat it! This gorgeous caramel is just for looks.

1 cup white Crayola Model Magic clay

1 (4-ounce) bottle white glue

1 to 2 tablespoons brown paint

3 drops yellow food coloring

1 cup shaving cream

1 tablespoon lotion

1 to 3 tablespoons Sta-Flo liquid starch

medium bowl

spoon

MAKE SOME FAUX SALT

1. Pinch off a little of your white clay and roll it into small little balls to create your salt.

2. Set the "salt" aside for about 10 minutes to let it harden.

MAKE CARAMEL

1. Pour your glue, paint, and food coloring into a medium bowl and mix to combine.

2. Add the shaving cream and lotion and mix to combine.

3. Activate your slime by stirring in the Sta-Flo until your slime forms.

4. Once your slime is completely mixed and no longer sticky, start folding in the clay until the slime no longer has lumps and has become smooth. Add more color if you need to.

5. Once the clay is fully incorporated, begin shaping your "caramel" into squares.

6. Last but not least, top your finished caramel with the salt you made earlier.

Honey Slime

This slime is enough to make the honey bees super jealous! Gooey, sweet, and luxurious, this is the perfect topping to any food-inspired slime.

1 (4-ounce) bottle clear glue

¼ cup water

2 drops brown paint

2 drops yellow food coloring

6 to 7 tablespoons clear liquid detergent

medium bowl

spoon

1. Pour the glue, water, paint, and food coloring into a medium bowl and mix to combine.

2. Slowly add in the detergent and mix to combine until your slime forms and holds its shape.

3. Once your slime is combined (it may still be slightly sticky), let it sit in the bowl at room temperature, covered with plastic wrap, for 1 to 5 days, until the bubbles disappear.

4. After the bubbles are gone, play with your Honey Slime or use it to dress up other food-inspired slimes.

Slime Hack

Make your slime thinner by adding more water.

STRAWBERRY JAM SLIME

Grape Jelly Slime

You can enjoy this popular jelly flavor not only on your toast, but now in slime form (but be sure not to eat it)!

1 (4-ounce) bottle clear glue

¼ cup water

3 or 4 drops purple paint

3 to 4 tablespoons clear liquid detergent

medium bowl

spoon

1. Combine the clear glue, water, and paint in a medium bowl and mix to combine.

2. Slowly add the detergent and mix until the slime forms and is no longer sticky.

3. Once your slime is fully mixed, let it sit in a bowl at room temperature covered with plastic wrap for 1 day, or until most bubbles are gone.

Strawberry Jam Slime

Strawberry slime is simple yet beautiful with its deep rich color and amazing smell.

1 (4-ounce) bottle clear glue

¼ cup water

4 or 5 drops red food coloring

1 drop strawberry essential oil

2 tablespoons black glitter

3 to 4 tablespoons clear liquid detergent

medium bowl

spoon

1. Pour the glue, water, food coloring, strawberry essential oil, and glitter into a medium bowl and mix to combine.

2. Slowly add the detergent and mix to combine until the slime forms and is no longer sticky.

3. Once all ingredients are combined and your slime is formed, let it sit in a bowl at room temperature covered with plastic wrap for a day or two, or until most of the bubbles are gone.

Chocolate Syrup Slime

Mouthwatering and rich, the sleek texture of chocolate syrup is found in this realistic replica. It even smells delicious! This tantalizing slime is the perfect addition to top any food-inspired slime.

1 (4-ounce) bottle clear glue

¾ cup water

½ cup shaving cream

1 drop chocolate essential oil

3 to 5 tablespoons clear liquid detergent

medium bowl

spoon

1. Mix the glue, water, shaving cream, essential oil, and food coloring in a medium bowl.

2. Slowly add the detergent and mix to combine until the slime forms.

3. Once your slime is combined, take it out and stretch it between your hands until it looks like chocolate syrup and is no longer sticky.

Slime Hack

Add more water to your slime to make a thinner "chocolate syrup."

Chocolate Pudding Parfait Slime

This chocolate parfait looks and smells so amazing, but don't let this delicious looking treat fool you—it's not real. Crazy, I know!

¼ cup tan craft sand

1 recipe Chocolate Soft-Serve Slime (see page 50)

1 recipe white Fluffy Slime (see page 103)

small colored Styrofoam balls (2 to 4 mm) (optional)

clear cup or container

spoon, for decoration

1. Pour the sand in the bottom of your container.

2. Add the Chocolate Soft-Serve Slime.

3. Place your Fluffy Slime on top and add sprinkles (colored balls) and a spoon for decoration!

CHOCOLATE PUDDING PARFAIT SLIME

Strawberry Parfait Slime

Feast your eyes on this bright and festive parfait of fun! With three layers of pure joy awaiting you, you won't know where to start.

¼ cup tan craft sand

1 recipe Strawberry Jam Slime
(see page 63)

1 recipe white Fluffy Slime
(see page 103)

small colored Styrofoam balls
(2 to 4 mm) (optional)

clear cup or container

spoon, for decoration

1. Pour the sand in the bottom of the container.

2. Add your Strawberry Jam Slime.

3. Place your Fluffy Slime on top and add sprinkles (colored balls) and a spoon for decoration. How cute!

Root Beer Float Slime

Inspired by the classic root beer float, but this one you can play with!

1 (4-ounce) bottle white glue

2 cups shaving cream

3 to 4 tablespoons lotion

6 to 8 tablespoons clear liquid detergent, divided

1 (4-ounce) bottle clear glue

¼ cup water

2 or 3 drops brown food coloring

2 medium bowls

3 spoons

glass or mason jar

MAKE ICE CREAM

1. Pour the white glue, shaving cream, and lotion into a bowl and mix to combine.

2. When the ingredients are mixed together, begin adding 3 to 4 tablespoons detergent and mix to combine until your slime has formed and is no longer sticky.

3. Once your slime has come together and is fluffy, set it to the side.

MAKE ROOT BEER

1. Pour the clear glue into a second medium bowl and then add the water and food coloring. Mix to combine.

2. Next, slowly add the remaining 3 to 4 tablespoons detergent until your slime holds it shape is no longer sticky.

ASSEMBLE THE FLOAT

1. Begin by placing your "root beer" into your glass.

2. Next, take your "ice cream" and place 1 to 2 scoops into your glass and push it halfway down.

3. Top your root beer float off with a spoon. Satisfy your senses by scooping your way around your slime float!

Key Lime Icy Float Slime

This slime looks very cold, but it won't freeze off your fingertips when you play with it. Enjoy the mixture of textures with this chilling slime.

1 (4-ounce) bottle white glue

2 cups shaving cream

3 to 4 tablespoons lotion

6 to 8 tablespoons clear liquid detergent, divided

1 (4-ounce) bottle clear glue

½ cup water

2 or 3 drops lime green paint

2 cups clear plastic beads (2 mm)

2 medium bowls

2 spoons

glass or mason jar

straw

MAKE SOME ICE CREAM

1. Pour the white glue, shaving cream, and lotion into a medium bowl and mix to combine.

2. When the ingredients are mixed together, begin adding 3 to 4 tablespoons detergent and mix until slime is combined and no longer sticky.

3. Once your slime has come together and is fluffy, set it aside side.

MAKE AN ICY

1. Pour the clear glue into a second medium bowl and then add the water and paint. Mix to combine.

2. Next, slowly add the remaining 3 to 4 tablespoons detergent until your slime has formed.

3. Once your slime has fully mixed and is still a little sticky, pour the beads into your slime and fold them in.

ASSEMBLY TIME

1. Begin by placing your "icy" into your glass.

2. Next, take your "ice cream," place it in the glass, and push it halfway down.

3. Top your Key Lime Icy Float Slime with a straw and enjoy poking your way through your new food-inspired slime.

Lemon Meringue Pie Slime

Mmmm...lemon meringue pie. This food-inspired dessert slime looks just like the real thing, but don't eat it!

1 cup white Crayola Model Magic soft clay

1 recipe yellow Jiggly Slime (see page 118)

1 cup shaving cream

1 mini pie mold

medium bowl

spoon

1. In a medium bowl, add the paint to the clay and blend it in until the clay becomes brown.

2. Press the clay into your mini pie mold.

3. Pour in enough Jiggly Slime to fill the mold.

4. Top with shaving cream and enjoy!

Candy Slime - EDIBLE

Choose your candy and grab some Marshmallow Fluff for this fun party slime!

Starbursts

jellybeans

Airheads

Gummi Bears

Swedish Fish

Skittles

mini marshmallows

Marshmallow Fluff

powdered sugar

large bowl

large spoon

1. Put as much candy and Marshmallow Fluff as you want into your bowl, and mix to combine.

2. Add powdered sugar to make the candy mixture less sticky, and dig in!

Soda Slime - EDIBLE

Do you like to play with your food before you eat it? Well, if so, this slime is for you. It is totally edible, super-simple, and delicious! Since this project involves using the microwave and very hot bowls, it's best to do make with the help of an adult.

1½ cups or 12 ounces soda (choose your favorite flavor)

3 tablespoons Metamucil

medium microwave-safe bowl

spoon

microwave

1. Stir together the can of soda and the Metamucil in a bowl.

2. Microwave the mixture on high for 30 seconds.

3. Carefully pull out the bowl and stir the mixture.

4. Again, microwave the mixture on high for 30 seconds.

5. Stir the mixture. Microwave on high for 30 seconds once more.

6. This time be very careful—the bowl will be hot! The mixture should be slime now and will need to sit and cool for about 10 minutes before handling.

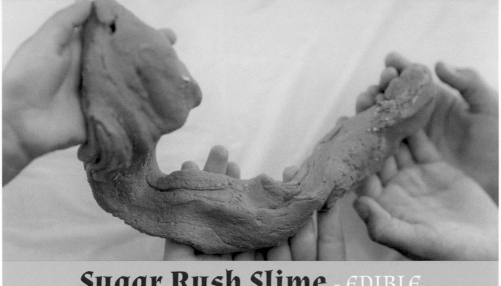

Sugar Rush Slime - EDIBLE

One bite of this edible slime will have you bouncing off the walls! Do you dare try it?

1 cup Marshmallow Fluff

1 (3-ounce) package Jell-O (sugar only)

2 to 3 cups powdered sugar

¼ cornstarch

medium bowl

spoon

1. Mix the Marshmallow Fluff, sugar from the Jell-O, powdered sugar, and cornstarch together in a bowl.

2. Have fun stretching and stealing nibbles from this sugary slime. What a rush!

Pantry Slime - EDIBLE

Who's hungry? Go check the pantry and see what you can pull out for this delicious snack-time slime. Let's eat!

Marshmallow Fluff

M&M's

graham crackers

Reese's Peanut Butter Cups

peanut butter

Nutella

sprinkles

powdered sugar

large bowl

large spoon

1. Put as much of each ingredient as you want into a large bowl and mix.

2. Enjoy your sweet and fluffy edible slime. Yum!

Marshmallow Dream Slime - EDIBLE

Fluffy slime that you can eat? Yes! This edible slime is so delicious, you will have to make more before the first one is even done. Since this project involves using the microwave and very hot bowls, it's best to make it with the help of an adult.

10 regular-sized marshmallows
1 cup powdered sugar
sprinkles

medium microwave-safe bowl
spoon
microwave

1. Microwave the marshmallows in a medium microwave-safe bowl on high for 30 seconds.

2. Stir the marshmallows and heat them for another 30 seconds on high.

3. Stir again. Caution: The bowl and marshmallows will be hot!

4. Let the mixture cool for about 5 minutes before handling.

5. Add the powdered sugar and mix thoroughly. Top off this delicious marshmallow slime with pretty sprinkles.

Chocolate Hazelnut Slime - EDIBLE

This slime is completely edible and tastes so good you may not have any left to play with. Eat up!

10 regular-sized marshmallows

½ cup Nutella

microwave

spoon

1. Microwave the marshmallows in a medium microwave-safe bowl on high for 30 seconds.

2. Stir the marshmallows and heat them for another 30 seconds on high.

3. Stir again. Caution: The bowl and marshmallows will be hot!

4. Add the Nutella and mix thoroughly.

5. When your marshmallows and Nutella are combined, let the mixture sit for about 5 minutes to cool before handling and consuming.

GLITTER SLIMES

Mermaid Scales Slime

Mermaids are enchanting and very beautiful. This slime glistens and shimmers just like a mermaid's tail when the light hits it just right. The depth of color is mesmerizing. Just one look and you'll be hooked!

½ (4-ounce) bottle clear glue

2 tablespoons water

1 tablespoon iridescent fine glitter

¼ cup green iridescent confetti glitter

2 to 3 tablespoons clear liquid detergent

medium bowl

spoon

1. Add the glue, water, fine glitter, and confetti glitter to a medium bowl and mix to combine.

2. Slowly add the detergent and mix until the slime forms.

3. Once your slime is no longer sticky, take it out of the bowl, stretch it, and enjoy its beauty.

Slime Hack

If your slime is cloudy and white, let it sit, covered with plastic or in a sealable container, for a few hours to a day to clear up some of the bubbles.

Add more glitter for even more sparkly fun!

Polka Dot Slime

Celebrate with this easy and exciting slime. The chunky glitter makes it adorable and loads of fun to stretch, poke, and swirl.

½ tablespoon baking soda

1 tablespoon contact lens solution

1 (4-ounce) bottle white glue

1 tablespoon colored chunky glitter

small bowl

spoon

medium bowl

1. Mix the baking soda and contact solution together in a small bowl. This will be your activator.

2. Pour the white glue and glitter into a medium bowl and mix to combine.

3. Slowly add the activator and mix to combine.

4. Once your slime has come together, pick it up and begin stretching it by hand.

5. As you stretch it, the slime will become less sticky. Time to poke a dot!

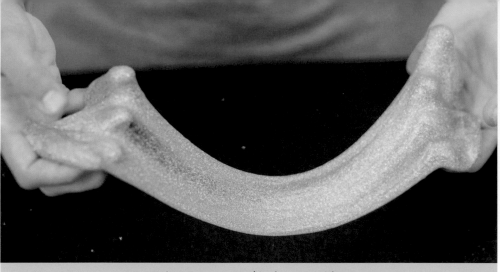

Holographic Slime

Loved for its reflectiveness and full bursts of color, this slime is a favorite among the slime community.

1 (4-ounce) bottle clear glue

¼ cup water

3 tablespoons fine holographic glitter

3 to 4 tablespoons clear liquid detergent

medium bowl

spoon

1. Pour the glue, water, and glitter into a medium bowl and mix to combine.

2. Slowly add the detergent and mix to combine until the slime forms and holds its shape.

3. Once your slime has come together, begin stretching it between your hands until it is no longer sticky.

Slime Hack

If your slime is a little sticky, add a little more detergent.

Glitter Bomb Slime

Glitter, glitter, glitter, and more glitter! You may find yourself mesmerized by this dazzling slime.

1 (4-ounce) bottle clear glue

¼ cup water

3 to 4 tablespoons clear liquid detergent

¼ cup glitter

medium bowl

spoon

1. Mix the glue and water together in a medium bowl.

2. Slowly begin adding the detergent a little at a time and mix to combine until the slime forms.

3. Once your slime is fully mixed and holds it shape, take it out and knead it with your hands until it is no longer sticky.

4. Use your hands to fold the glitter into your slime. A glitter bomb masterpiece!

Slime Hack

If your slime is lumpy, don't worry. Add a little water and let it sit for an hour or two. It will absorb the water and relax. Once it is the consistency you wish, finish by adding the glitter.

For clearer slime, set your finished slime to the side, covered tightly with plastic wrap for 3 to 5 days at room temperature until the bubbles disappear, and then add the glitter.

Princess Slime

Perfect for any little princess, this slime shimmers and shines with unmatched beauty. It's like a magical iridescent fairy tale!

1 (4-ounce) bottle clear glue

¼ cup water

½ cup iridescent small glitter

¼ cup manicure glitter

3 to 4 tablespoons clear liquid detergent

medium bowl

spoon

1. Mix the glue and water together in a medium bowl.

2. Add both glitters and mix to combine.

3. Slowly add the detergent and mix to combine until the slime comes together and holds its shape.

4. Once your slime is fully mixed, let it sit for 3 to 5 days, covered with plastic wrap at room temperature, until it becomes clear.

Slime Hack

Try placing your clear slime in front of a window if it's not too hot. The bubbles will clear up faster.

Ballerina Slime

Sweet, adorable, and lovely are all ways to describe little ballerinas. Those words also apply to this sparkly, glitter-filled slime. It is full of shimmer and it shines when the light hits it, much like the costumes of a ballerina.

½ recipe Basic Slime #1 (see page 19) or Basic Slime #2 (see page 19)

2 to 4 drops light pink food coloring

1 recipe Clear Slime (see page 20)

1 tablespoon white holographic chunky glitter

1 tablespoon white holographic fine glitter

clear sealable container

2 medium bowls

spoon

1. First, put the Basic Slime into a bowl and mix in the pink food coloring. Set aside.

2. In a second bowl, fold the glitter into your Clear Slime and set aside.

3. Now place the Clear Slime at the bottom of your container. It should go no higher than three-fourths of the way up the sides.

4. Place the pink slime on top of the Clear Slime and push down lightly. After covering your container with a lid or plastic wrap, let the slime sit and transform for 2 to 5 days at room temperature. If using plastic wrap, make sure it doesn't touch the slime. The pink slime will fall and create "ruffles," just like a ballerina's tutu.

Confetti Pop Slime

Pop, crunch, and snap goes the slime!

1 (4-ounce) bottle white glue

2 cups shaving cream

1 cup large confetti glitter

medium bowl

spoon

1. Combine the glue and shaving cream in a medium bowl and mix.

2. Add the contact lens solution and mix until your slime comes together and is slightly sticky.

3. Add the glitter and fold it in with your hands.

4. Enjoy this satisfying slime right away, or place it back into the bowl, cover it with plastic wrap, and let the bubbles rise for a day. Once the bubbles have risen, you can experience the ultimate pop, crunch, and snap of this amazing slime.

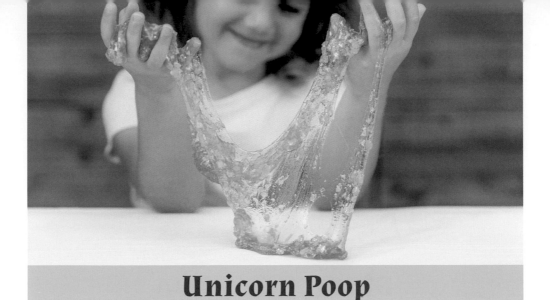

Unicorn Poop

What goes in must come out...eww, gross! Unicorn poop is in fact the most amazing-looking poop you will ever see!

1 recipe Clear Slime (see page 20)
1 drop blue food coloring
1 tablespoon fine iridescent glitter

1 tablespoon medium iridescent glitter
1 tablespoon chunky iridescent glitter
medium bowl

1. Add the food coloring to the Clear Slime. Use your hands to fold the color in until your slime is blue.

2. Add the glitter and fold it in with your hands as well. Enjoy your mesmerizing Unicorn Poop. See, it's not gross at all! Quite the opposite, really.

Unicorn Slime

Named after the mystical creature, this slime has become legendary with its magical, shimmery, iridescent charm.

1 recipe Clear Slime (see page 20)
1 tablespoon fine iridescent glitter
1 tablespoon medium iridescent glitter

1 tablespoon chunky iridescent glitter
medium bowl
spoon

1. Place the Clear Slime in a medium bowl and slowly fold in the glitter. Try to avoid making bubbles.

2. Once all the glitter is folded in, you are done and ready to be mesmerized.

Black Hole Slime

Black as night and full of sparkling, shimmering glitter, this slime is a holographic delight!

1 (4-ounce) bottle clear glue

1 or 2 drops black paint

2 tablespoons black glitter

2 tablespoons holographic glitter

3 to 5 tablespoons clear liquid detergent

medium bowl

spoon

1. Pour the glue, paint, black glitter, and holographic glitter into a medium bowl and mix to combine.

2. Slowly add the detergent and mix until the slime holds its shape. Stretch the slime between your hands until it is no longer sticky. Add more glitter if you wish, and enjoy this galactic delight!

Ocean Jewel Slime

This slime's smooth iridescence mimics the glisten of sunlight hitting calm ocean water.

1 recipe Clear Slime (see page 20)

1 or 2 drops aqua blue food coloring

2 tablespoons fine iridescent glitter

shallow dish

spoon

1. Place your Clear Slime into a shallow dish and fold in the food coloring to color your slime blue. Try not to create too many bubbles.

2. Sprinkle the glitter on top and fold it in.

Cameron's Midnight Slime

This slime is rich in color and shimmers like the moonlight.

1 (4-ounce) bottle clear glue

2 to 4 drops blue food coloring

1 teaspoon iridescent glitter

2 to 3 tablespoons Sta-Flo liquid starch

medium bowl

spoon

1. Combine the glue, food coloring, and glitter in a medium bowl and mix to combine.

2. Add the Sta-Flo a little at a time and stir until your slime is completely mixed and holds its shape.

3. Take your slime out of the bowl and knead and stretch it until it is no longer sticky. Enjoy this midnight surprise.

Cameron's Fluffy Midnight Slime

This playful, fluffy slime shimmers—squeeze it once and you'll be hooked!

1 (4-ounce) bottle clear glue

2 cups shaving cream

12 drops blue food coloring

3 teaspoons iridescent glitter

5 to 7 tablespoons Sta-Flo liquid starch

medium bowl

spoon

1. Combine the glue, shaving cream, food coloring, and glitter in a medium bowl and mix.

2. Add the Sta-Flo a little at a time and stir until your slime forms and holds a fluffy, bouncy shape.

3. Take your slime out of the bowl and knead and stretch it until it is no longer sticky.

Galaxy Slime

This galactic slime is a definite crowd-pleaser with all its glorious glitter and color combinations. Galaxy slime is a true out-of-this-world experience!

1 (4-ounce) bottle white glue

2 drops purple food coloring

2 drops pink food coloring

2 drops blue food coloring

1 cup various colors and sizes of glitter

3 to 5 tablespoons clear liquid detergent

3 small bowls

spoon

1. Divide the glue evenly among three small bowls.

2. Drop a different color into each bowl and sprinkle in the glitter.

3. Slowly add the detergent to each bowl and stir until your slimes form and hold their shapes.

4. Once your slimes are no longer sticky, place them side by side and explore the galaxy.

CAMERON'S FLUFFY MIDNIGHT SLIME

Fluffy Galaxy Slime

This pumped-up galactic slime will bring a smile to your face. You might even feel like you're a million light-years away from Earth while you poke and stretch your way through this fluffy slime.

1 (4-ounce) bottle white glue

2 cups shaving cream

1 cup foaming hand soap

1 or 2 drops purple food coloring

1 or 2 drops pink food coloring

1 or 2 drops blue food coloring

1 cup various colors and sizes of glitter

6 to 7 tablespoons liquid detergent

spoon

3 small bowls

1. Divide the glue evenly among three small bowls.

2. Divide the shaving cream and foaming soap evenly among the three bowls. Add different food coloring to each bowl. Sprinkle in some glitter and mix to combine.

3. Slowly add detergent to each bowl and stir until your slime forms and holds its shape.

4. Once your slimes are no longer sticky, place them side by side and immerse yourself in your fluffy galaxy.

GLUE-FREE SLIMES

Oobleck Slime

Oobleck is not a slime, but just as awesome. Is it a solid or a liquid? That remains the question. What do you think?

1 cup water

5 drops food coloring of choice (optional)

1¾ cups cornstarch

medium bowl

spoon

1. Pour the water into a medium bowl and add the food coloring, if using, and mix to combine.

2. Add the cornstarch and mix to combine. You may have to get your hands dirty.

3. The oobleck should be hard when you tap it and your finger should sink into it if you lay it on top. If your oobleck is too dry, add a little more water. If it's too wet, add a little more cornstarch.

Microwave Toothpaste Slime

It may sound crazy, but it works. Because the bowls and materials used in this slime get super-hot in the microwave, this one is better to make with an adult.

2 tablespoons gel/paste toothpaste

microwave

small microwave-safe bowl

spoon

1. Add the toothpaste to a small microwave-safe bowl and microwave on high for 5 to 10 seconds. Take it out and stir. Caution—it will be hot.

2. Repeat this process until your toothpaste is slime. Let it sit in the bowl for 5 to 10 minutes until cool enough to pick up and stretch.

Slime Hack

If your slime is still sticky after it's made, add a teaspoon of baby oil to get rid of the stickiness.

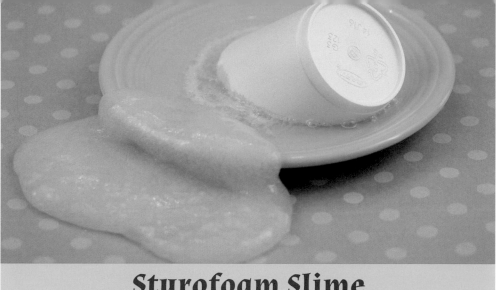

Styrofoam Slime

What if you could make smooth slime with just a cup and acetone (a.k.a. nail polish remover)? Now you can. This insane slime is made right before your eyes. It takes just a few minutes and there is no mixing required.

1 cup 100% pure nail acetone

Styrofoam cup

1. Pour the acetone in a shallow dish and hold the Styrofoam cup inside the acetone. It will bubble and shrink.

2. When the cup has completely disintegrated, you will be left with slime.

Carefully pull the slime out of the acetone and enjoy stretching and bending it.

3. Be sure to wash your hands after making and playing with this slime.

Caution:
Acetone is a chemical and will remove the color or finish off clothes, furniture, and almost anything. This slime is to be made *with* adult supervision.

SHAMPOO SLIME

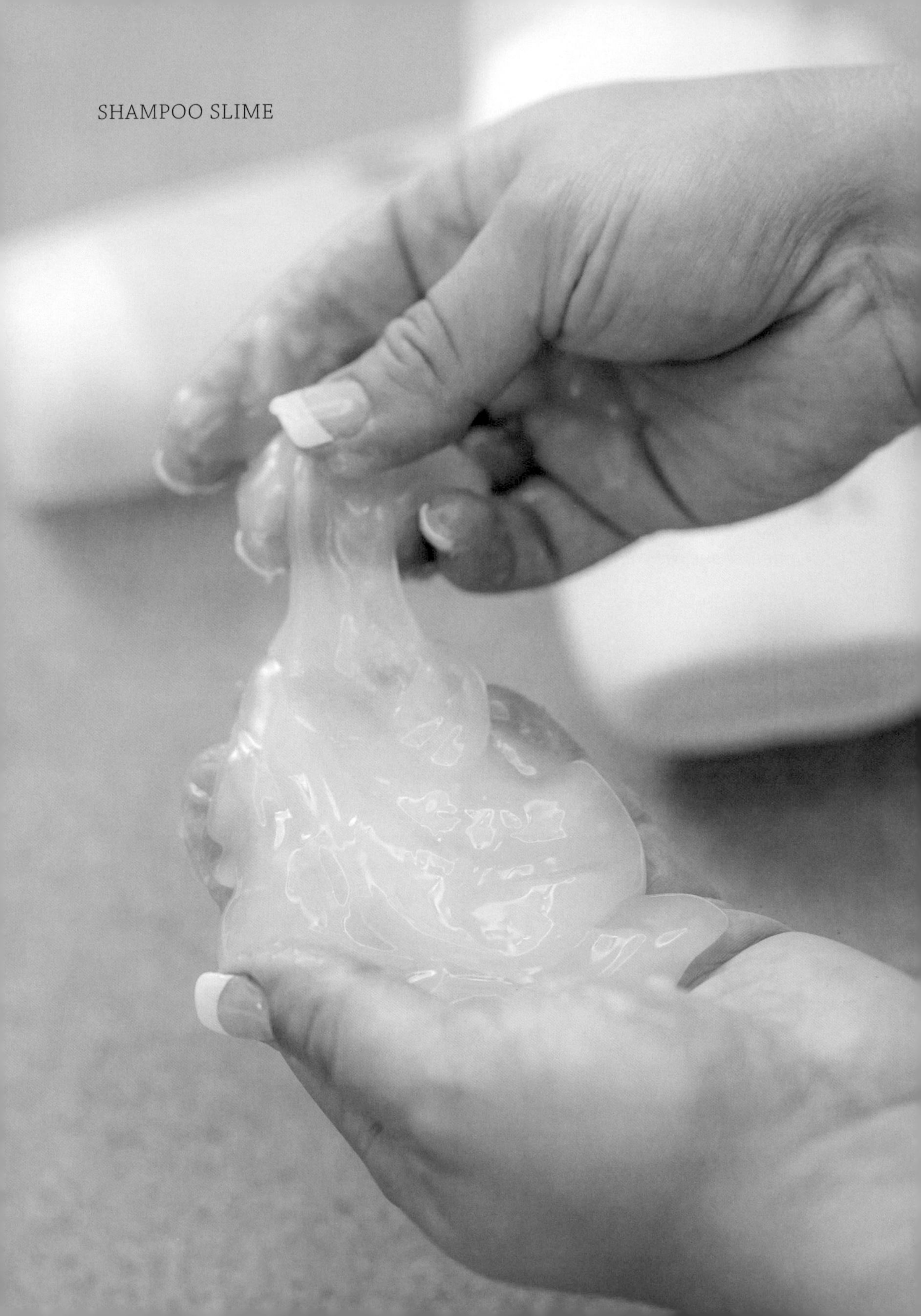

Shampoo Slime

If you had to choose between washing your hair or making slime, which would you choose? Can't decide? OK then, let's do both! Yep, let's make slime that you can use, and you don't even have to leave the shower.

2 tablespoons 3-in-1 shampoo
1 tablespoon body wash

small bowl
spoon

1. Add the shampoo and body wash to a small bowl and mix to combine.

2. Scrub up!

Lotion Slime

This two-ingredient slime could not get any easier or feel any more amazing. You'll want to play with it for days!

½ cup white Crayola Model Magic soft clay
1½ tablespoons lotion

small bowl
spoon

1. Knead the lotion and clay together in a small bowl. This might be messy to start, but it will come together quickly.

2. You're done! Enjoy the buttery texture.

Clay-Free Clay Slime

Got a hankering for some clay slime, but fresh out of clay? No problem! Get the smooth feel of clay slime with ingredients you already have at home.

2 tablespoons conditioner

1 or 2 drops food coloring of choice

2 to 3 tablespoons cornstarch

small bowl

spoon

1. Mix the conditioner and food coloring together in a small bowl.

2. Add the cornstarch and mix until it becomes a little crumbly.

3. Use your hands to knead the mixture. You should notice it becoming smoother and more slime-like. Once you have reached this consistency, you can enjoy stretching and playing with it.

Fluffy Clay Slime

This fluffy slime is amazing because you only need two ingredients and it doesn't require glue. The fluffy texture of this slime is so enjoyable to squeeze and mold to any shape. Hours of fun are sure to be had!

½ cup white Crayola Model Magic soft clay

2 cups shaving cream

1. Start by laying out the clay on a flat surface and then adding the shaving cream 1 cup at a time.

2. Mix with your hands until each cup is incorporated thoroughly.

Flour Slime

Bored? Have nothing to do? Make this easy no glue slime. It's fun and sure to please.

¼ cup flour

2 tablespoons water

3 drops food coloring of choice
(optional)

small bowl

spoon

1. Mix the flour and water together in a small bowl.

2. Mix in food coloring, if using. It's that easy. Have fun!

Slime Hack

If your slime is too thick, add a little water.
If it's too soupy, add more flour.

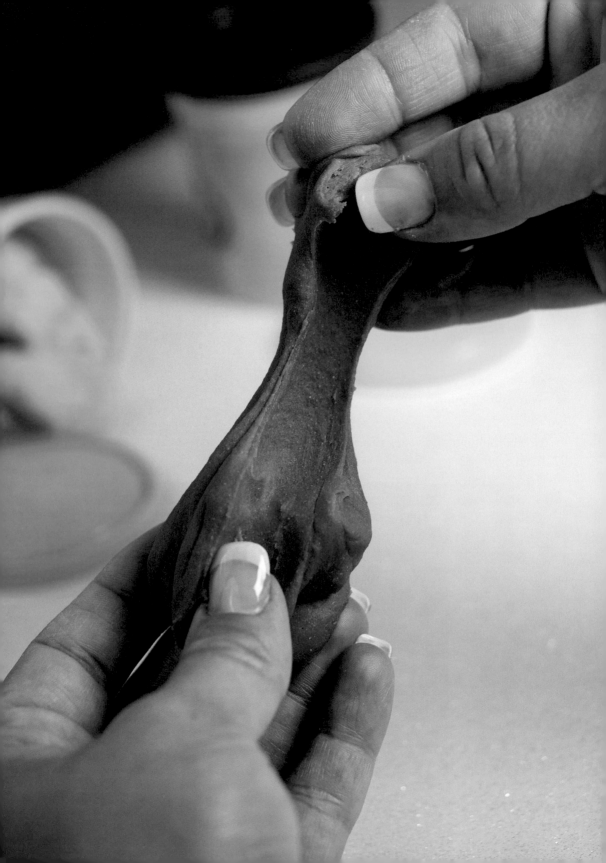

Dough Slime

What if you could take the texture of Play-Doh and make it even softer? Well, you can. It's easy! This slime is so soft and smooth, you won't want to put it down.

1 (5-ounce) tub Play-Doh

1 tablespoon lotion

nonstick plate

1. Start by flattening out the Play-Doh and placing it on a nonstick plate.

2. Make a well in the center and begin adding the lotion.

3. Combine using your hands until all the lotion is incorporated.

VIRAL
SLIMES

Fluffy Slime

Let's get crazy! Put some bounce into your basic slime. This amazingly soft slime feels so squishy as it glides through your hands as you squeeze.

1 (4-ounce) bottle white glue
3 to 5 drops food coloring of choice
2 cups shaving cream

3 tablespoons contact lens solution
medium bowl
spoon

1. Pour the glue and food coloring into a medium bowl and mix to combine.

2. Add the shaving cream and stir.

3. Slowly add the contact lens solution while mixing. Once your slime has formed, it should be fluffy. Continue stretching it by hand until it is no longer sticky.

Slime Hack

To make the slime less sticky, mix ½ teaspoon baking soda and 2 tablespoons water together. Fold into the slime as needed.

"Why is my Fluffy Slime not working?" This is a common question that we hear. Fluffy Slime is not fluffy unless you add enough shaving cream. So, if this is the problem, just add more. You also must add enough activator, which in this case is the contact lens solution.

Bubbly Rainbow Slime

You won't find a pot of gold or a Leprechaun at the end of this rainbow, but you will find a sense of satisfaction when you pop these airy bubbles.

2 (4-ounce) bottles white glue

4 cups shaving cream

1 cup foaming hand soap

½ cup plus 2 tablespoons Sta-Flo liquid starch

2 drops each color red, orange, yellow, green, blue, and purple food coloring

large bowl

6 medium bowls

spoon

large rectangular container, for storage

MAKE THE BASE

1. Combine the glue, shaving cream, and foaming soap in a large bowl and mix.

2. Add the Sta-Flo a little at a time, until the slime is formed and fluffy.

ADD COLOR

1. Fold in the color. Use 1 color per slime.

MAKE THE RAINBOW

1. Place the slime into the rectangular container in rainbow order: red, orange, yellow, green, blue, and purple.

2. Place the lid on the container and let the slime sit for 1 to 5 days at room

3. Once your slime is fully mixed and not sticky, divide it into 6 equal parts in separate medium bowls.

temperature. The longer you leave it, the higher the bubbles will rise.

3. The slime will transform into a beautiful bubbly rainbow paradise. When you're ready, delight your ears with the satisfying sound of bursting bubbles.

Clear Rainbow Slime

See clear to the other side with this rainbow!

1 (4-ounce) bottle clear glue

¼ cup water

3 to 5 tablespoons clear liquid detergent

1 or 2 drops each color red, orange, yellow, green, blue, and purple food coloring

6 small bowls

medium bowl

spoon

1. Combine the glue and water in a medium bowl and mix.

2. Add the detergent a little at a time until the slime forms.

3. Once your slime has formed, knead it with your hands until it becomes less sticky.

4. Cover your slime with plastic wrap and let it sit for 3 to 5 days at room temperature to clear up, or move on to coloring your slimes.

5. Once you're ready, divide your slime among 6 small bowls and add food coloring to each one. When you're done, line them up side by side and begin stretching and swirling your colorful rainbow.

Bubble Solution Slime

This slime makes HUMONGOUS bubbles! Who doesn't want to have fun with that?

1 (4-ounce) bottle clear glue

½ cup bubble solution

5 tablespoons Sta-Flo liquid starch

5 drops food coloring of choice (optional)

medium bowl

spoon

1. In a medium bowl, slowly mix together the clear glue and bubble solution. You don't want to make bubbles just yet.

2. Add the your Sta-Flo and mix until slime is formed and holds its shape.

3. Take your slime out of the bowl and begin kneading it with your hands until it's no longer sticky.

4. Now get ready to make HUGE bubbles. This will work best if you do it with a friend. Hold the corners of the slime, slowly stretch it out, and then begin bringing it up and then down. You should see a big bubble in the middle after a few times of repeating the up and down motion. Isn't that awesome? Who wants to be in the bubble first?

Slime Hack

If your slime begins to get sticky, simply add a little more Sta-Flo.

Clay Slime

This slime is perfect for swirling because it keeps its moldable form, yet is soft and smooth enough to spread with a butter knife. One of the most popular slimes online, this is often referred to as Butter Slime.

1 (4-ounce) bottle white glue

5 drops food coloring of choice

1 cup shaving cream

2½ tablespoons clear liquid detergent

2 cups white Crayola Model Magic soft clay

medium bowl

spoon

1. Mix the glue and food coloring together in a medium bowl.

2. Add the shaving cream and mix to combine.

3. Stir in the detergent.

4. Once your slime is fully mixed, continue kneading it by hand.

5. When it is no longer sticky, begin adding the clay. Knead the clay into your slime until it is well incorporated.

6. Stretch, swirl, and enjoy this buttery slime.

Toothpaste Slime

Toothpaste isn't just for your teeth anymore. I know, crazy! It can, in fact, be made into a minty fresh slime.

white glue

gel/paste toothpaste

spoon

medium bowl

1. In a medium bowl add the toothpaste and the glue in a 1-to-1 radio.

2. Now whip it up!

Metallic Pearl Slime

Now, for some real drama. This is no common slime. Its brilliant color puts it a cut above all the rest. This slime's dimension, texture, and brilliance demand attention, and that is exactly what it gets.

1 (4-ounce) bottle clear glue

¼ cup water

3 to 5 tablespoons clear liquid detergent

½ teaspoon pearl or metallic pigment powder

medium bowl

spoon

1. Mix the glue and water together in a medium bowl.

2. Slowly add the detergent and mix to combine until the slime holds its shape.

3. Once your slime has come together, begin kneading with your hands.

4. Lay your slime out on a nonstick surface and sprinkle the metallic powder over it.

5. Fold the slime over the powder and repeat until the powder is completely encased and has colored your slime.

Color-Changing Slime

This epic slime changes from one color to the next. It's the perfect addition to your slime collection! Note that you'll want to be careful not to inhale the fine powder used in this slime. Adult supervision is recommended.

1 recipe Clear Slime (see page 20)

2 teaspoons thermochromic pigment powder

shallow dish

1. Place the Clear Slime in a shallow dish and add the thermochromic powder.

2. Fold the powder into the slime using your hands until it is completely incorporated.

3. Use the heat from your hands to change the color.

Slime Hack
Use an ice cube to cool the slime.

GLOW-IN-THE DARK SLIME

Glow-in-the Dark Slime

Don't have a flashlight? That's OK, take your slime! Problem solved.

½ tablespoon baking soda

1¼ tablespoons contact lens solution

1 (4-ounce) bottle white glue

2 tablespoons glow-in-the-dark paint

flashlight or lamp

small bowl

spoon

medium bowl

1. Mix together the baking soda and contact lens solution in a small bowl. This will be your activator. Set it aside.

2. Pour the glue into a medium bowl and add the glow-in-the-dark paint. Mix thoroughly.

3. Next, slowly add the activator. Mix until the slime forms and holds its shape.

4. Take it out of your bowl and begin kneading it by hand until it is no longer sticky.

5. Finally, charge the slime by placing it under a flashlight or lamp for about 1 minute. Move the flashlight so that the whole surface of the slime is charged.

6. Find a dark room and enjoy the show!

Fluffy Glow-in-the-Dark Slime

Glowing slime—made even cooler with glowing bubbles!

1 (4-ounce) bottle clear glue

¼ cup water

2 cups shaving cream

4 tablespoons glow-in-the-dark paint

6 to 7 tablespoons clear liquid detergent

flashlight or lamp

medium bowl

spoon

1. Pour the glue, water, shaving cream and glow-in-the-dark paint into a medium bowl and mix thoroughly.

2. Slowly add the detergent and mix thoroughly until the slime begins to form and holds its shape.

3. Take it out of the bowl and begin kneading it by hand until it is no longer sticky.

4. Let this slime sit in a bowl covered with plastic wrap for a day until bubbles form. Don't let the plastic wrap touch the slime.

5. Charge the slime by placing it under a flashlight or lamp for about 1 minute and moving the light over the surface of the slime. Take it into a dark room and explore its array of glowing bubbles.

Magnetic Slime

It's alive! Well, not really, but it sure looks like it is. This is by far my favorite slime. All you need is a neodymium (rare earth) magnet to bring the coolest of all slimes to life. Note that is important not to inhale the fine black iron oxide powder used in this slime. Adult supervision is required.

½ tablespoon baking soda

1 tablespoon of contact lens solution

1 (4-ounce) bottle white glue

1 tablespoon black iron oxide powder

neodymium magnet

spoon

medium bowl

small bowl

1. Mix the baking soda and contact solution together in a small bowl. This will be your activator.

2. Pour the glue into a medium bowl and add the activator. Mix together until the slime begins to form.

3. When your slime has formed, begin kneading it by hand until it becomes less sticky.

4. Fold in the iron oxide powder using your hands. Once all the powder is incorporated, pick up a magnet and watch your slime really move.

Slime Hack

Add more iron oxide powder to see if it makes the slime move faster.

Rare earth magnets aren't all that rare. You can get one at a craft store.

Avalanche Slime

This may be the prettiest of all the slimes, and it comes from Instagram user @Honey.Guts. This beauty is so magical, otherworldly even. Once it's made, let it sit somewhere for all to see and watch in amazement as it transforms.

1 recipe Clear Slime (see page 20)

1 or 2 drops two different food colorings of choice

1 tongue depressor or small spoon

½ recipe white Basic Slime #1 (see page 19) or Basic Slime #2 (see page 19)

clear sealable container

1. Place the Clear Slime (must be free of bubbles) at the bottom of a clear sealable container. It should go no higher than three-fourths of the way up the sides.

2. On one side of the container, lightly add a drop of one of your food colorings.

3. Take your second food coloring and do the same thing on the other side of the slime.

4. Use a tongue depressor or spoon and push down gently on the sides of your slime so that the color moves down on all the sides of your container.

5. Place the Basic Slime on top of your Clear Slime and close the container.

6. Let this slime sit at room temperature and transform for 2 to 5 days. The white slime will fall and create the most beautiful shapes. Once you are done staring and taking pictures, take your amazing slime out to play!

AVALANCHE SLIME

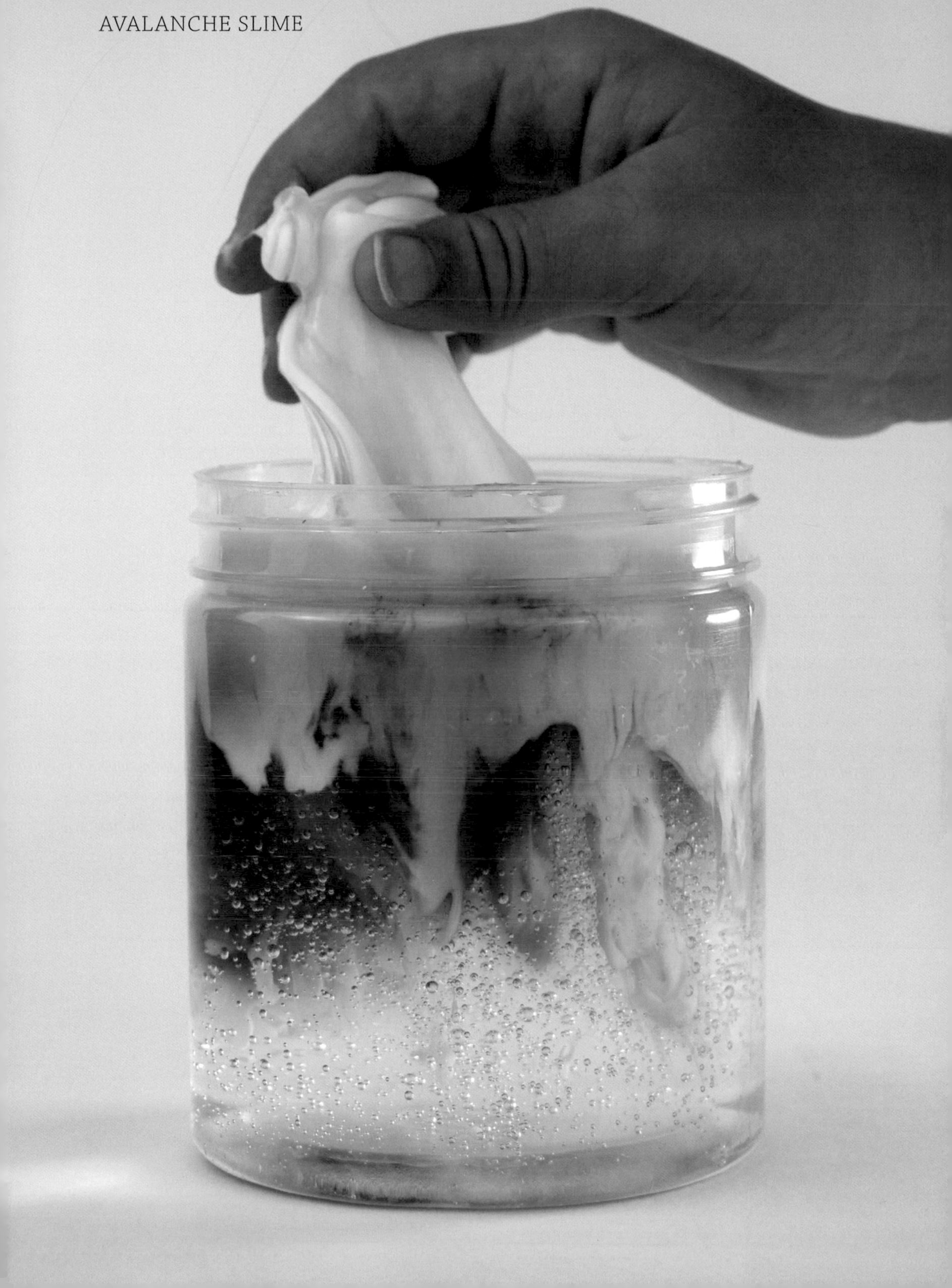

Lava Slime

This slime features an eerie appearance thanks to its ever-changing depths of color.

1 recipe Basic Slime #1 (see page 19) or Basic Slime #2 (see page 19)

1 or 2 drops red food coloring

3 or 4 drops black paint

1 recipe Clear Slime (see page 20)

clear sealable container

1. Separate your Basic Slime in half. Place each half on a flat surface. Using your hands, fold the red food coloring into one half. Using your hands, fold the black paint into the second half.

2. Place your black slime at the bottom of a sealable container and then top it with the Clear Slime (which should have no bubbles). Together they should go no higher than three-fourths of the way up the sides.

3. Put the red slime on top of the Clear Slime. You should have black on the bottom, clear in the middle, and red on top.

4. Cover the slime with the container lid and let it sit at room temperature and transform for 2 to 5 days. The black slime will rise to the top and the red will sink to the bottom, creating a hot-lava effect.

Animal House Millefiori Slime

Pictures in slime? Who would have thought? Create an eye-catching animal slime with these adorable clay disks of animals. Millefiori is a technique that produces decorative patterns in glass or clay. Millefiori beads made from polymer clay can be purchased online. You can also buy millefiori canes and cut your own beads, although this requires adult supervision.

1 (4-ounce) bottle clear glue

¼ cup water

3 to 4 tablespoons clear liquid detergent

2 tablespoons animal-patterned millefiori disks

shallow dish

medium bowl

spoon

1. Pour the glue and water into a medium bowl and mix to combine.

2. Slowly add in the detergent and mix until the slime forms.

3. Cover with plastic wrap or place your slime in a sealable container. Set aside for 3 to 5 days at room temperature for it to clear up. After the bubbles are gone, it is time create your Animal House!

4. Take a shallow dish and place your slime in it. Now fold in the millefiori disks.

Jiggly Slime

It's alive! This slime comes to life with fun, interactive jiggles.

1 (4-ounce) bottle white glue
2 drops food coloring of choice
1½ cups water, divided

5 to 6 tablespoons Sta-Flo liquid starch
medium bowl
spoon

1. Mix the glue, food coloring, and ¼ cup of the water in a medium bowl.

2. Add the Sta-Flo and mix until your slime forms and holds its shape.

3. Take the slime out of the bowl and knead with your hands until it is no longer sticky.

4. Place the slime back into the bowl, add some of the remaining water, and poke it a few times.

5. Let the slime rest a few minutes to absorb the water.

6. Do this a few times until all the water is used.

7. Once your slime has absorbed all the water, it's time to wiggle and jiggle.

Clear Jiggly Slime

See-through liquid glass slime is so cool. Make it jiggle, and it is awesome!

2 (4-ounce) bottles clear glue

4 drops food coloring of choice

2 cups water, divided

6 tablespoons clear liquid detergent

large bowl

spoon

1. Mix the glue, food coloring, and ½ cup of the water in a medium bowl.

2. Add the detergent and mix until the slime is formed and holds its shape.

3. Take the slime out of the bowl and knead with your hands until it is no longer sticky.

4. Place the slime back into the bowl, add some of the remaining water, and poke it a few times.

5. Let the slime rest a few minutes to absorb the water.

6. Do this a few times until all the water is used. Once your slime has absorbed all the water, it will come together and jiggle. Let it sit for 3 to 5 days at room temperature in the bowl, covered with plastic wrap, to become super clear and jiggly.

Smooth Matte Slime

If you want a smooth matte finish on your slime, this is the one for you!

2 (4-ounce) bottles white glue

¼ cup water

2 cups cornstarch, divided

1 cup shaving cream

2 tablespoons lotion

10 tablespoons Sta-Flo liquid starch

large bowl

spoon

1. Combine the glue, water, 1 cup of the cornstarch, shaving cream, and lotion in a large bowl and mix thoroughly.

2. Add the remaining 1 cup cornstarch and mix again.

3. Slowly add the Sta-Flo, stirring after each tablespoon.

4. Once your slime holds its shape, you will be left with a rich, creamy, and satisfying slime, just waiting to be poked! Due to the large amount of cornstarch in this slime, store it in the refrigerator for longevity.

Slime Hack

After your slime is completed, add baby oil to rid it of any stickiness.

Fluffy Jiggly Slime

Fluffy jiggles make this slime irresistible. It dances when your poke it!

2 (4-ounce) bottles white glue

5 to 7 drops food coloring of choice

2 cups shaving cream

1 cup water, divided

8 to 9 tablespoons Sta-Flo liquid starch

medium bowl

spoon

1. Mix together the glue, food coloring, shaving cream, and ¼ cup of the water in a medium bowl.

2. Add the Sta-Flo and mix until the slime is formed and holds its shape.

3. Take the slime out of the bowl and knead with your hands until it is no longer sticky.

4. Place the slime back into the bowl, add some of the remaining water, and poke it a few times.

5. Let the slime rest a few minutes to absorb the water.

6. Do this a few times until all the water is used. Once your slime has absorbed all the water, it's time to dance and jiggle.

Slime Hack

If you want your slime to jiggle even more, add more water.

Glossy Slime

Glossy slime is so much fun to play with. It's sleek and smooth like colored glass and tricks the eye with its wet appearance.

1 (4-ounce) bottle white glue

2 to 3 tablespoons clear glue

2 drops food coloring of choice

1 teaspoon lotion

3 tablespoons Sta-Flo liquid starch

medium bowl

spoon

1. Pour the white and clear glue into a medium bowl.

2. Add the lotion and food coloring and mix to combine.

3. Slowly add the Sta-Flo and mix to combine.

4. When your mixture is thoroughly mixed and holds it shape, take it out of the bowl and begin kneading it between your hands until it is no longer sticky.

Slime Hack

Let this slime sit for a couple days at room temperature in a sealed container to really see the shine.

Stained-Glass Slime

The transparency of this slime resembles stained glass, but it won't break if you drop it.

1 (4-ounce) bottle clear glue

¼ cup water

2 drops paint or food coloring of choice

4 to 5 tablespoons Sta-Flo liquid starch

medium bowl

spoon

1. Pour the glue, water, and color into a bowl and mix to combine.

2. Slowly add the Sta-Flo and mix until the slime forms.

3. When your slime is mixed thoroughly, take it out of the bowl and begin kneading with your hands until it is no longer sticky. Let this slime sit at room temperature for a couple days in a sealed container for maximum shine. It's amazing!

Slime Hack

For thinner slime, add more water.

GLOSSY SLIME

Pool Party Slime

Summer is full of fun: family vacations, friends, beaches, traveling, and, best of all, slime! Not just any slime either—a colorful pool party. Grab your pool rings and let's make some waves!

2 drops of blue food coloring

1 recipe Clear Jiggly Slime (see page 119)

20 colorful ring beads, rainbow looms bands (small colorful rubber bands), or colorful Styrofoam balls

large bowl

clear sealable container

1. In a large bowl, fold the blue food coloring into the Clear Jiggly Slime.

2. Place the slime in a clear container and top it with colorful rings beads or rainbow loops ("life preservers"), or Styrofoam balls ("beach balls"). Once you're done playing with the slime, place the lid on the container and set it aside at room temperature.

Super-Stretchy Slime

You won't believe the stretch in this slime—it makes a contortionist look stiff!

2 (4-ounce) bottles white glue

¼ cup water

1 tablespoon body wash

1 cup shaving cream

1 cup foaming hand soap

1 teaspoon baby oil

8 to 10 tablespoons Sta-Flo liquid starch

7 drops food coloring of choice (optional)

large bowl

spoon

1. Pour the glue, water, body wash, shaving cream, hand soap, baby oil, and food coloring, if using, into a large bowl and mix together.

2. Slowly add the Sta-Flo and mix until the slime forms.

3. Knead the slime by hand and enjoy poking and playing with its amazing stretchiness!

Plaster Slime

You may not be able to fix the walls with this slime, but it will keep you from climbing them. It's smooth and stretchy to the touch, making it super soothing.

1 (4-ounce) bottle white glue

¼ cup Plaster of Paris

1 tablespoon liquid detergent

medium bowl

spoon

1. Pour the glue and plaster into a medium bowl and mix to combine.

2. Slowly add in the detergent and mix until the slime forms and holds its shape.

3. Take the slime out of the bowl and knead until smooth.

Clicky Slime

The interaction of clear and white glue makes the ultimate clicky slime with amazing-sounding clicks that will leave you more than satisfied.

½ (4-ounce) bottle clear glue

½ (4-ounce) bottle white glue

1 or 2 drops food coloring of choice

4 tablespoons Sta-Flo liquid starch

medium bowl

spoon

1. In a medium bowl, mix together the clear glue, white glue, and food coloring.

2. Slowly add in the Sta-Flo and mix until the slime is formed and holds its shape.

3. Once your slime is formed, stretch it between your hands until it is no longer sticky.

4. Place the slime on a nonstick surface and poke it to hear the "click, click, clicks."

Slime Hack

Want a little sparkle? Add some glitter to your slime.

ABOUT THE AUTHOR

On YouTube, **Adam Vandergrift** is known as "Will It Slime?" but at home, he is simply Daddy. He is a husband, and a father to three adorable daughters, ages four, six, and ten. His journey with slime began when his young daughters wanted to get creative one afternoon. The girls, who are homeschooled, are interested in crafting, science experiments, and anything fun! Slime making has been a fun project that is enjoyed as a family. Mixing together a few ingredients and witnessing the transformation into slime while hearing the laughter and excitement of his daughters has been such a joy for Adam.

Adam first created the YouTube channel "Will It Slime?" after noticing that slime was a growing trend on Instagram. At that time, it had only a small presence on YouTube, so he decided to create a channel devoted solely to slime. In addition to making slime, Adam used creative editing, sound effects, and upbeat music to make the channel even more interesting and exciting for viewers, which made the channel as distinctive and unique as possible. "Will It Slime?" has grown to become the largest channel on YouTube dedicated to slime.

Be sure to look for "Will It Slime?" on YouTube. Follow Adam on Instagram and Facebook @willitslime, and visit his website www.willitslime.com.

CLICKY SLIME